# MORE PUDDLE QUESTIONS FOR CANADIAN SCHOOLS

GRADE 3

## Assessing Mathematical Thinking


### Authors

**Elizabeth Ainslie**
Toronto, Ontario

**Paula Dodick**
Toronto, Ontario

**Deborah Karam**
Toronto, Ontario

**Helen Laruccia**
Toronto, Ontario

**Helen Mason**
Harwood, Ontario

**Brian McCudden**
Toronto, Ontario

**Yvonne O'Neill**
Port Hope, Ontario

**Rochelle Williams**
Toronto, Ontario

### Advisors

**Dale Armstrong**
Edmonton, Alberta

**Sherry Bennett**
Calgary, Alberta

**James Hansen**
Victoria, British Columbia

**Robin Harris**
Halifax, Nova Scotia

**Anne MacLeod**
St. John, New Brunswick

**Heather Syms**
Halifax, Nova Scotia



McGraw-Hill Ryerson

Toronto Montréal Boston Burr Ridge, IL Dubuque, IA Madison, WI New York San Francisco St. Louis Bangkok Beijing Bogotá Caracas Kuala Lumpur Lisbon London Madrid Mexico City Milan New Delhi Santiago Seoul Singapore Sydney Taipei

COPIES OF THIS BOOK MAY BE OBTAINED BY CONTACTING:

McGraw-Hill Ryerson Ltd.

WEB SITE:
*http://www.mcgrawhill.ca*

E-MAIL:
*orders@mcgrawhill.ca*

TOLL-FREE FAX:
1-800-463-5885

TOLL-FREE CALL:
1-800-565-5758

OR BY MAILING YOUR ORDER TO:
McGraw-Hill Ryerson
Order Department
300 Water Street
Whitby, ON L1N 9B6

Please quote the ISBN and title when placing your order.

The McGraw·Hill Companies

McGraw-Hill Ryerson

*More Puddle Questions for Canadian Schools, Grade 3*



ISBN: 0-07-090667-X

*http://www.mcgrawhill.ca*

1 2 3 4 5 6 7 8 9 10 M 10 9 8 7 6 5 4

Printed and bound in Canada



**National Library of Canada Cataloguing in Publication**

More puddle questions for Canadian schools : assessing mathematical thinking / Elizabeth Ainslie ... [et al.].

ISBN 0-07-090664-5 (grade 1).-- ISBN 0-07-090666-1 (grade 2).--
ISBN 0-07-090667-X (grade 3)

1. Mathematics--Study and teaching (Primary). 2. Mathematics--Problems, exercises, etc. I. Ainslie, Elizabeth

QA139.M67 2003 372.7'044 C2003-904923-X

Publisher: Diane Wyman
Developmental Editor: Helen Mason
Reginal Rubrics Editors: Maggie Cheverie, Jean Ford
Manager, Editorial Services: Linda Allison
Supervising Editors: Cathy Deak, Crystal Shortt
Editorial Assistant: Erin Parton Hartley
Copy Editor: Mary Agnes Challoner
Production Manager: Yolanda Pigden
Electronic Page Make-Up: Sharon Lucas
Cover and All Other Illustrations: Francisco Creative Images
Cover Design: Sharon Lucas
Interior Design: Greg Devitt

# Table of Contents

## Acknowledgements

The authors and editors of *More Puddle Questions for Canadian Schools* wish to thank the field-test teachers listed below, and their students, for their thoughtful comments and suggestions.

### Field-Test Teachers

Heather Caron
Toronto District School Board

Suzanne Cameron
Toronto Catholic District School Board

Peggy Cyra
Toronto Catholic District School Board

Paula Cziranka
Kawartha Pine Ridge District School Board

Julie DiNunzio
Toronto Catholic District School Board

Lorelei Eccleston Dart
Toronto District School Board

Gayle Freedman
United Synagogue Day School

Amy Gowland
Toronto District School Board

Claudette Goddar
Toronto District School Board

Miya Kinos-Goodin
Avalon East District School Board

Anna Intarakosit
Toronto District School Board

Heather Johnson
Hamilton-Wentworth District School Board

Lesley Jenkins
Hamilton-Wentworth District School Board

Debbie Karam
Toronto Catholic District School Board

Zsolt Kecskemeti
Toronto Catholic District School Board

Lee-Anne Knox
Kawartha Pine Ridge District School Board

Brenda Leonard
Kawartha Pine Ridge District School Board

Alison Lam
Toronto District School Board

Gwenna McWhinnie
Toronto District School Board

Sonia Poradzisz
Toronto Catholic District School Board

Patricia Sellar
Hamilton-Wentworth District School Board

Rod Simpson
Avalon East District School Board

Kathleen Schratz
Toronto District School Board

Consuella Tabone
Toronto Catholic District School Board

Tanya Volcke
Toronto Catholic District School Board

Helena Watt
Toronto Catholic District School Board

Dawn Watters
Kawartha Pine Ridge District School Board

Geoffrey Winship
Toronto District School Board

## Dear Teacher,

*The original Puddle Questions were so popular with teachers that we have decided to develop a set of Puddle Questions geared specifically to Canadian provincial curricula. This book contains ten new Puddle Questions that cover key concepts of Canadian provincial curricula. Each new Puddle Question is accompanied by a rubric that shows which mathematics expectations are being addressed, and several student exemplars that show different ways students have attempted to answer each question.*

*This book contains rubrics aligned to the Ontario assessment standards. Rubrics aligned to the Western Canadian Protocol and Atlantic Provinces Education Foundation assessment standards are included on the enclosed CD-ROM.*

*We worked with a group of primary teachers and Math consultants to develop a new set of Puddle Questions to challenge and to excite primary students. Once we had developed the questions, we piloted them in classrooms throughout the province. Some classes had already worked with Puddle Questions. Others had not. We used feedback from both types of classrooms to develop the exemplars and rubrics that you see in this resource.*

*Like the developers of the original Puddle Questions, we were fascinated by the variety of unique ways students found to solve the problems and present their thinking on paper. We used their responses to help us revise the rubrics. We also revised some of the questions and retested them to see if the new wording and visuals worked better to get students working with curriculum expectations.*

*It was interesting to compare these reactions and results to what happened in classes where problem solving is part of regular class work. There, students seemed to thrive on the problems. They used a variety of strategies — some of them ingenious — and produced work that exceeded our expectations. These students demonstrated powerful mathematical thinking and were able to communicate their ideas effectively.*

*We hope that you get as much joy as we have from seeing students grow in their ability to solve rich and complex problems.*

Puddle Questions Advisors

## Presenting the Problems

### The Teacher's Role

With Puddle Questions, as with open-ended assessment in general, the teacher acts as a facilitator in the problem-solving process. Teachers distribute the problem pages and introduce the problem briefly by reading it aloud. (Blackline masters of the problem pages in both English and French are provided on **pages 77–96**.) Students need to understand that you want to see their best work, and their most careful thinking. They should know that there is no one right answer to the problem. Students should also know how they will be evaluated. For each problem, assessment criteria are listed in the Presenting the Problem section of the teaching notes. You can also ask students the questions found in Prompts for Getting Started.

While the students work on the problems, you can reread the Prompts for Getting Started questions, either to individuals or to the whole group. This will help remind students of aspects of the problem they may not have attended to at first, but that may be more pertinent as they get deeper into the problem.

Your most important role, while the students are working on Puddle Questions, is to monitor and observe the students while they work through the problem by themselves. Note what strategies students attempt, whether they can use the strategy to come up with an answer, how many different strategies they explore, and how well they record what they are doing. Try not to direct their work into one avenue or another. Give the students time to come up with their own ideas.

### Time Period

It is important to be flexible with the amount of time allowed for Puddle Questions. Some questions may take 45–60 minutes. Others may work best if done over several days. Although this may seem an extended period of time for such a problem, the richness of the task will provide students with a lot of experience working with parts of the mathematics curriculum.

Ideally, students should be allowed to work on the problems as long as they want to. They may wish to work for a while, and then revise their papers or start again.

### Materials

Choosing the proper tools is part of the solution process. Students should have access to any reasonable tools or equipment they need to solve the problem. Calculators, manipulatives (such as linking cubes or Base Ten Blocks) and measuring devices (such as rulers or scales) should be readily available. Ideally, the classroom should have a large assortment of these and other manipulatives that students can use whenever they feel the need.

The important thing is to avoid dictating what tools the students should use. For example, distributing graph paper for a problem might give the false impression that graph paper must be used for a correct solution. A better method is to have available a range of standard equipment from which students can choose. A list of tools and materials is provided in the introduction to each problem.

## CD-ROM

This provides rubrics aligned to the Western Canadian Protocol and Atlantic Provinces Education Foundation assessment standards.

## The Students' Role

In most problems, students are asked to write a report to explain their thinking and reasoning, to draw pictures or sketches of their plans, or to display data in some way. Let the students use their own invented spellings for words they do not know.

If work is difficult to decipher, you may want the student to read the paper to you so that you can understand what is being said. Some students may tape-record their ideas. Students can also dictate their ideas for you, or an aide, to write on their papers. Alternatively, allow students to use computer software.

In Puddle Questions, we are asking students to take responsibility for doing their best work and for showing what they know. This mirrors real life. There, tasks are often not spelled out. Thinking through a problem, making a choice, and then following through, are all parts of the problem-solving process.

Sometimes, people are expected to present their ideas thoughtfully. At other times, they must communicate in a way that gives others a clear understanding of the thinking involved. Often, people are expected to display information in interesting and easily understandable ways. The same expectations exist in the classroom.

You can help students keep these things in mind by giving them a copy of the Problem Solving model on **page 97**. This gives students some guidelines as they write up their reports for the investigations. The page could be stapled for their math portfolios and referred to each time they do an investigation. It could also be used as an overhead transparency and displayed while the students work on a problem.

## Problem Solving Model

A visual of the Problem Solving Model is on **page 97**. The chart on the next page reviews what to look for at each step. Remind students that problem solving is a circular process. At any stage in the process, they can either return to an earlier stage or move ahead to a later stage.

## Self-Assessment

On the students' problem page is a self-assessment tool. Students are to shade the tool to show the level at which they feel they performed in the investigation. It is interesting to compare students' self assessment scores to the scores they receive from you for the investigation. You might want to discuss discrepancies between the two, should they occur.

| Stage | What You Are Looking For | Student Wording |
|---|---|---|
| 1 | That students understand the problem. | 1. **Think.** Make sure you know what the problem is all about. |
| 2 | That students select an appropriate plan for solving the problem. | 2. **Plan.** Think of strategies to try. Select an appropriate plan. |
| 3 | That students carry out their plan. | 3. **Do.** Solve the problem. |
| 4 | That students look back to examine the solution. | 4. **Look back.** Think about and talk about how you solved the problem. |
| 5 | That students can communicate their thinking. | 5. **Communicate.** Explain your work clearly using words, pictures, and numbers. |

## Assessing the Work

### How to Score Holistically

We recommend using a holistic approach for scoring the responses to the Puddle Questions. In a holistic approach, you look at the work globally and give one overall score to the response, rather than giving points for various aspects of the response. The emphasis should be on thinking skills, mathematical understanding, and reasoning, rather than on use of arithmetic or computational techniques.

A student who has made arithmetic errors might receive a high score because of the depth of mathematical thinking that the response shows. Conversely, a student with accurate computation may receive a low score because the response does not show an understanding of mathematical ideas. Exceptional scores are reserved for the one or two responses that show a certain amount of finesse. You may find that no student's response fits in this category for some Puddle Questions.

There are many ways to score your students' work. Consider using one of the following methods:

- The scoring rubric provided with the problem. This rubric provides four levels of response to the specific problem in the investigation. The levels follow the assessment levels in Canadian assessment standards: Levels 1, 2, 3, 4. Sometimes student work does not reach Level 1. In this case, it should not be scored when using Ontario assessment standards. The rubrics in this book use Ontario assessment standards. The teacher CD-ROM provided with this book includes assessment rubrics for the Western and Eastern provinces. Each of these rubrics follows the assessment criteria of the specific provinces.

- Your district's own scoring rubric or a scoring rubric of your choice. Many school boards have established their own assessment schemes and scoring rubrics.
- Your own scoring technique.
- A revision of the general scoring rubric developed for your own class or for specific student needs.

| Category | Statement | Evidence |
|---|---|---|
| All categories | Amount of assistance needed | 1. a lot<br>2. some<br>3. none —independent<br>4. none —independent |
| Problem Solving | Number of strategies and how used | 1. a limited range<br>2. some appropriately<br>3. several appropriately<br>4. a variety appropriately |
| Understanding of Concepts | Number of concepts seems to understand | 1. a few<br>2. some<br>3. most<br>4. almost all |
| Application of Mathematical Procedures | Number and kinds of errors and omissions | 1. major<br>2. some minor<br>3. few minor<br>4. practically none |
| Communication | Clarity and precision of communication | 1. unclear<br>2. some clarity<br>3. clear<br>4. clear and concise |
| | Amount and use of math terminology | 1. rarely uses appropriately<br>2. uses some appropriately<br>3. usually uses appropriately<br>4. almost always uses appropriately |

As you consider student work, the following chart will assist you in identifying the level that students are at.

It is also useful to work with students to develop and post problem solutions. Then, students can consider and discuss the various strategies different students used and consider the usefulness of each strategy.

When assessing student work, look for strategies such as the following.

| Strategy | Students' Work | What You Might Teach |
|---|---|---|
| 1. Use objects. | Students use manipulatives to provide a concrete way to represent the solution. | 1. Model using manipulatives in various ways.<br>2. Encourage students to use manipulatives. Have them explain their thinking as they do so. |
| 2. Draw a picture. | Students use a sketch to illustrate the information in the problem. | 1. Model rough sketches that show all required information. |
| 3. Make a graph or table. | Students organize the information in a graph or table to identify what is missing. | 1. Provide a lot of experience reading, completing, and constructing graphs and tables. |
| 4. Look for a pattern. | Students identify and explain a pattern as they solve the problem. | 1. Provide a lot of experience in pattern recognition.<br>2. Provide a lot of experience reading tables and graphs. |
| 5. Look for all possibilities. | Students systematically identify all possible solutions. | 1. Encourage students to consider another way a problem might be solved. |
| 6. Guess and check. | Students consider what they know and guess at answers, then check. | 1. Encourage students to make educated guesses by asking them what they know and how this might affect their guess.<br>2. Model guessing and checking by thinking aloud about what you know about the sample problem and how this might affect the guess. |
| 7. Choose the operation(s) | Students decide whether to add, subtract, multiply, or divide, and then do it. | 1. Model using manipulatives to help decide which operation to use.<br>2. Discuss key words that suggest each operation. |
| 8. Solve a simpler or similar problem. | Students simplify the problem and solve it. | 1. Model thinking about how to simplify problems to check that a strategy works. |
| 9. Use logical thinking. | Students use known facts to look for relationships and get new information to solve a problem. | 1. Encourage students to reflect upon and share their strategies. |

## Student Exemplars

Sample responses for Levels 1, 2, 3, and 4 are shown with each problem. Some responses were gathered during the winter term (February 2003). No doubt the same students would have done different work at different times. The responses used in this book are intended to be typical of the level they represent. In order to provide good examples, we sometimes developed composite responses using aspects from more than one piece of work.

The exemplars are guides to help you score student work. It is not possible to represent here the full range of responses for these types of problems. However, studying these samples will give you an idea of the variety of ways students can solve the problems. The samples may also help you score your class responses by providing one or two benchmarks for each level.

In addition, the explanation with the samples may help you understand why it was assessed the level it was. These tips may help you to assess the level of thinking in student work.

## Making Observations

The scoring rubric gives only one part of what you learn from a student's work on the investigations. To obtain a more complete picture, you will want to make anecdotal records of your observations about how students tackled the problems, and what you learned about what they know. This can be done on plain note paper, 3" x 5" cards, or on the special Observation Checklist provided on **page 98.**

Your observations should focus on these aspects of the students' work habits:

- the amount of assistance needed;
- whether, and how well, manipulatives were used; and
- how well they collaborated with others.

You might want to focus your observations on one of these areas each time you do an investigation.

## Portfolios

Students can keep their investigation reports in a special portfolio. This way, they can see improvement over the year in their ability to tackle open-ended problems. These portfolios are also useful for parent conferences. Authentic assessment is often very useful in showing parents what students can and cannot do.

## Consolidation of Learning

### Reflection

The Puddle Questions are intended to be more than just an evaluation of what students can do. They are supposed to be a learning experience. Reflection is an important part of learning. After students have worked on a Puddle Question, it is a good idea to have them see and discuss sample responses developed within the class. Students can then see what others have done and listen to each others' thinking.

### Using Exemplars

If exemplars are discussed in a general way when students report on their thinking, students can pick up ideas and use these to modify their own responses. Encourage a number of students to discuss and share the work they did and the variety of ways they solved the problem.

Each problem has several suggestions for class discussions. The key is to let students explain their thinking to each other. In doing so, they may (1) realize that they were misdirected in their reasoning, or (2) help others understand how they might have done the problem differently.

### Follow-Up Activity

The follow-up activity described for each problem is a natural outgrowth of the investigation itself. Its purpose again is to extend the learning experiences inherent in the problem situation. These activities usually take one class period to complete.

## Ideas for Customizing a Scoring Rubric

Use the ideas on the next page as pointers if you wish to develop a customized rubric for each Puddle Question.

# General Scoring Rubric

## Level 1

Needs assistance.
Uses a limited range of appropriate strategies.
Provides partially complete and inappropriate explanations.
Uses only a few of the required concepts.
Applies basic problem-solving procedures.
Fails to address significant aspects of the problem.
Has major errors and/or omissions.
Communicates poorly; does not explain thinking.

Rarely uses appropriate math terminology

## Level 2

Needs limited assistance.
Uses appropriate strategies.
Provides appropriate but incomplete explanations.
Uses more than half of the required concepts.
Applies appropriate problem-solving procedures.
Addresses some aspects of the problem.
Has several minor errors and/or omissions.
Communicates with some clarity; begins to explain thinking.

Sometimes uses appropriate math terminology

## Level 3

Works independently.
Chooses the most appropriate strategies.
Provides appropriate and complete explanations.
Uses most required concepts.
Applies the most appropriate problem-solving procedures.
Addresses significant aspects of the problem.
Has a few minor errors and/or omissions.
Communicates clearly; explains thinking.

Usually uses appropriate math terminology.

## Level 4

Works independently.
Modifies known strategies or creates new ones.
Provides complete and appropriate explanations that show originality and creativity.
Uses all required concepts.
Applies the most appropriate strategies and justifies choices.
Has almost no minor errors and/or omissions.
Communicates clearly, precisely, and confidently.
Always uses appropriate math terminology.

INVESTIGATION 1

# The Jelly Bean Problem

**Focus: Number Sense and Numeration**

In this investigation, students are challenged to find ways of determining the number of jelly beans in two jars. One jar clearly holds more than the other does. Students are challenged with the task of finding as many different ways as they can to find the total number. In order to do this, they must use their problem-solving skills and think of a variety of strategies.

## Curriculum Expectations

- Represent whole numbers using concrete materials, drawings, numerals, and number words.
- Understand and explain basic operations involving whole numbers by modelling and discussing a variety of problem situations.
- Select and perform computation techniques appropriate to specific problems and determine whether the results are reasonable.
- Solve problems and describe and explain the strategies used.
- Justify in oral or written expression the method chosen for addition and subtraction; include reference to estimation, mental computation, concrete materials, or calculators.
- Use a calculator to solve problems beyond the required pencil-and-paper skills.
- Read and print numerals from 0 to 1000.
- Count by 1s, 2s, 5s, 10s, and 100s to 1000 using various starting points and by 25s to 1000 using multiples of 25 as starting points.
- Identify and describe numbers to 1000 in real-life situations to develop a sense of number.
- Use appropriate strategies to solve number problems involving whole numbers.
- Use various estimation strategies to solve problems, then check results for reasonableness.

## Prior Knowledge/Skills

Students will have been exposed to a number of counting strategies. Before doing this activity, they should have experience with:

- counting by 5s, 10s, and 25s in a large variety of contexts;
- "counting on" from a number;
- estimating if an amount is more than 10 or more than 100;
- comparing two numbers; and
- using multiplying as a strategy for finding "how many."

Prior to trying this activity, model communication by numbers, words, and pictures for students. Provide students with a variety of opportunities to communicate in written form using more than just numbers.

## Materials

blank paper
pencils and crayons

## Grouping Arrangement

Introduce the problem in a large group. Students will work individually on the task.

# Presenting the Problem

1. Tell the students that they are going to do a question that will let them show what they know about numbers. Start by displaying a large collection of objects (around 100). Ask students: "Is this more than 10 or less than 10? Is it more than 50 or less than 50? Is it more than 100 or less than 100? How do you know?"
2. Read the problem to the class. Describe the picture to them.
3. Clarify that their job is to write how to find the number of jelly beans there would be in the jars. Confirm that the picture in this problem shows a real thing. To show them, have two jars with some objects in them in the classroom.
4. Remind students that they should tell as many ways as they can. They can use pictures, words, and numbers.
5. Review the assessment criteria with the students.

## Assessment Criteria

It is important to let students know what they will be evaluated on before they start their task. Tell them that you are interested in having them:

- describe different strategies for counting;
- consider how to estimate the number of jelly beans;
- communicate these strategies; and
- use words, numbers, and pictures as effective ways of communicating.

## Prompts for Getting Started

Some students initially may have difficulty getting started in their thinking. Others may feel that they are done after having presented only one strategy. Some prompts to help them continue in their investigation include:

- What do you see in the picture? What are you trying to find out? (Clarify that they understand the question.)
- Pretend that you are telling your little sister or brother how to do the counting. What would you say?
- Pretend that you are telling a classmate how to estimate the number of jelly beans. What might you suggest?
- How might your friend do this question?
- Explain to me, orally, how you might find how many jelly beans are here. (Listen to the oral explanation, provide encouragement, and then challenge the student to try to put on paper exactly what was just said.)

## Assessing the Work

Students should suggest many different strategies for finding the total number of jelly beans in the two jars. Possible strategies include:

- estimating,
- counting,
- sorting,
- massing,
- tallying, and
- counting one layer and multiplying,

### Hints for Scoring a Response

Student responses are being assessed for the level of mathematical understanding they represent. As you assess each response, consider the following questions:

- Did the student need assistance to get started?
- Did the student need assistance to complete the task?
- Did the student draw or indicate groups of 10's or 25's?
- Did the student relate the number from one jar to the number in the other jar?
- Did the student estimate the answer?
- Did the student suggest "counting on" from the number in one of the jars?
- Did the student suggest emptying the two jars into a pile and then counting?
- Did the student have other suggestions for finding the number of jelly beans — perhaps eating them one by one!

## Scoring Rubric

See page 18.

## Consolidating Learning

1. Provide students with the opportunity to "show and tell" their work to the other students. Allow all students a chance to show one of their methods.
2. As a student is showing one solution, ask the rest of the group: "How many of you did it this way?"
3. As students explain their strategies, identify the strategy for the rest of the class. If the class has a "strategy wall" (similar to a word wall), then post any new strategies. This works exceptionally well if the student who suggested the method is acknowledged. For example, you might post: "Tara's strategy was to count by 5's."

## Follow-Up Activity

1. Provide real jelly beans or small objects of a similar size in a Mason™ jar. Ask students to find as many ways of measuring the jelly beans as they can.
2. Provide students with jelly beans or objects of a similar size. Have them bring in various packages and pour the jelly beans or other objects into each package. Ask them to compare their results and make conclusions.

INVESTIGATION 1

# The Jelly Bean Problem Rubric

Name____________________ Date__________

| Expectations | Level 1 | Level 2 | Level 3 | Level 4 |
|---|---|---|---|---|
| **Problem Solving**<br><br>3m4, 3m7, 3m8, 3m13, 3m32, 3m33 | With assistance, selects a strategy. | With some assistance, selects a strategy. | Selects a few strategies. | Selects several appropriate strategies. |
| **Understanding of Concepts**<br><br>3m1, 3m10, 3m11, 3m13 | Demonstrates limited understanding of quantities less than approximately 100. | Demonstrates some understanding of quantities less than approximately 100. | Demonstrates general understanding of quantities less than approximately 100. | Demonstrates an in-depth understanding of quantities less than approximately 100. |
| **Application of Procedures**<br><br>3m8, 3m9, 3m10 | Attempts a strategy in an unorganized way (e.g., by pointing to beans). | Attempts a strategy in a partially organized way (e.g., by colouring the beans as counts). | Uses strategies efficiently (e.g., by grouping as counts). | Uses innovative strategies efficiently and clearly. |
| **Communication**<br><br>3m8, 3m9, 3m17 | Communication is unclear, imprecise, or incomplete. | Communication has some clarity but may be incomplete. | Communication is clear and complete, using math terms and symbols. | Communication is clear and precise, with several ways of explaining using math terms and symbols. |

• See CD-ROM for additional regional rubrics.

Comments:

### Level 4 Response

This student has used a number of strategies, including estimating, counting, grouping, massing, and using a tally chart. The response shows a number of quite sophisticated methods. The communication is clear and concise. Note the use of words and visuals.

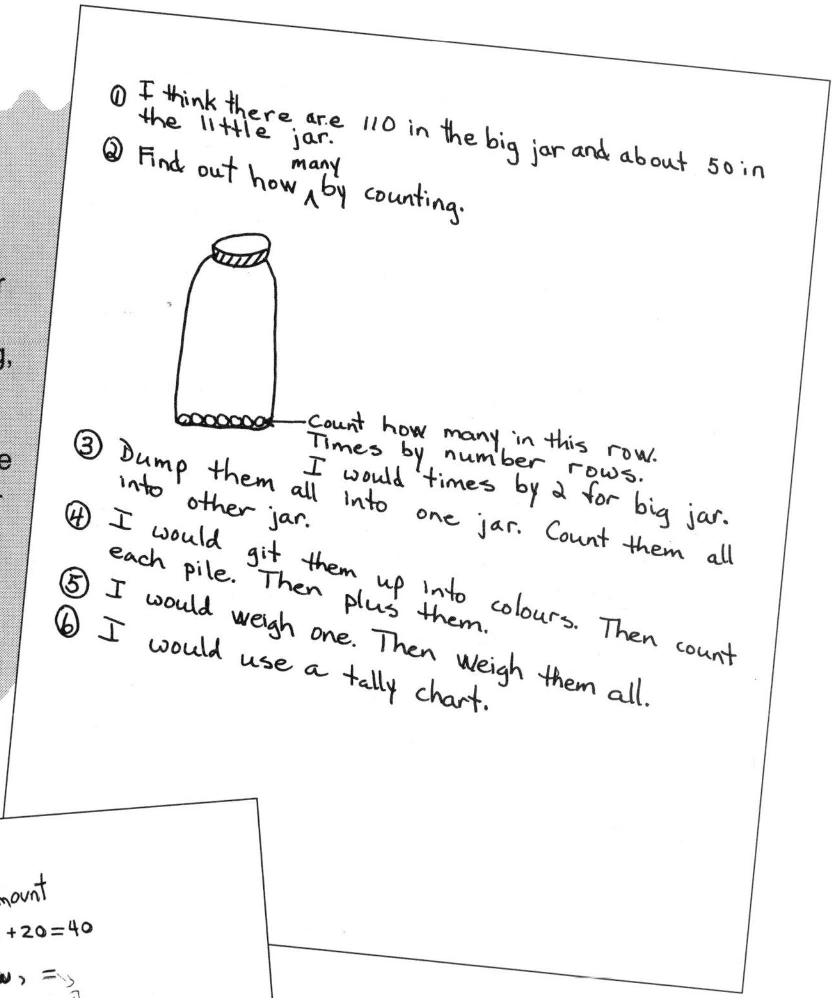

① I think there are 110 in the big jar and about 50 in the little jar.
② Find out how many by counting.

Count how many in this row. Times by number rows. I would times by 2 for big jar.

③ Dump them all into one jar. Count them all into other jar.
④ I would git them up into colours. Then count each pile. Then plus them.
⑤ I would weigh one. Then weigh them all.
⑥ I would use a tally chart.

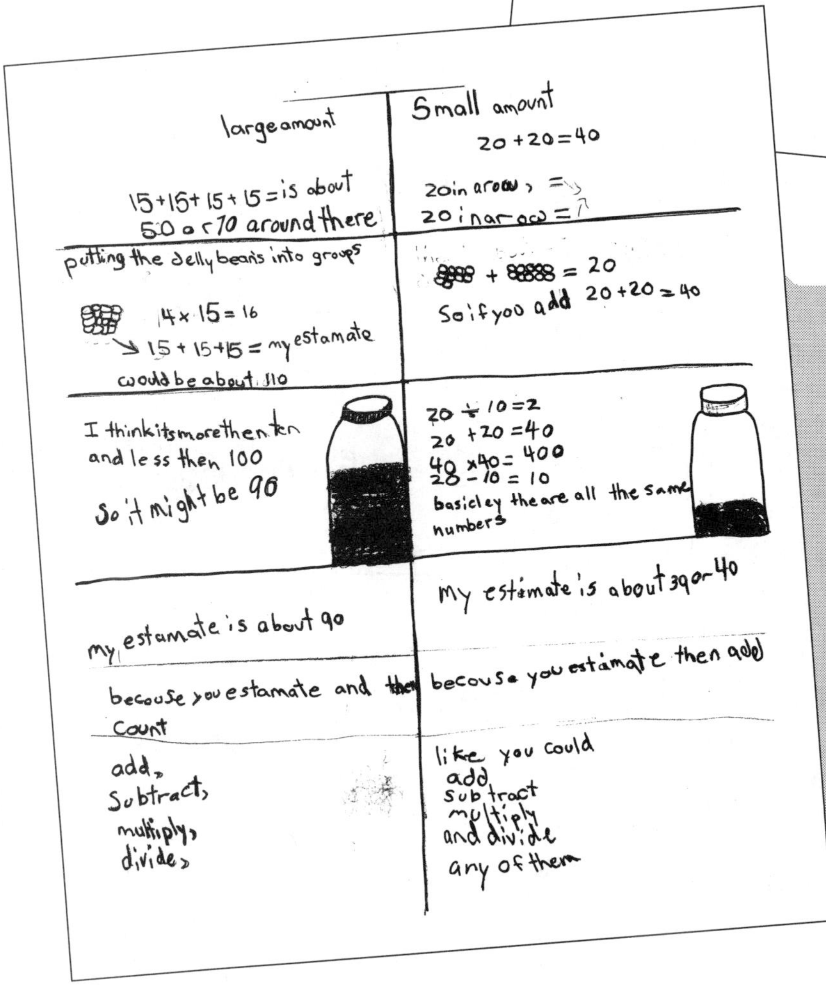

| largeamount | Small amount |
|---|---|
| 15+15+15+15=is about 50 or 70 around there | 20+20=40<br>20in arow =<br>20inarow = |
| putting the delly beans into groups<br>14×15=16<br>15+15+15= my estamate would be about 110 | + = 20<br>So if you add 20+20=40 |
| I thinkits more then ten and less then 100<br>So it might be 90 | 20÷10=2<br>20+20=40<br>40×40=400<br>28−10=10<br>basicley the are all the same numbers |
| my estamate is about 90 | My estimate is about 39 or 40 |
| becouse you estamate and then count | becouse you estimate then add |
| add,<br>Subtract,<br>multiply,<br>divide, | like you could add subtract multiply and divide any of them |

### Level 3 Response

This student uses a number of strategies, including grouping and adding, and estimating. She also recognizes the possibility of using other strategies, such as subtracting, multiplying, and dividing. The response shows what is in *each* jar. The communication uses words, pictures, and symbols. There are some inaccuracies.

### Level 2 Response

This student uses two problem-solving strategies: estimating and counting. The communication is simple and somewhat clear. The response uses words, visuals, and symbols.

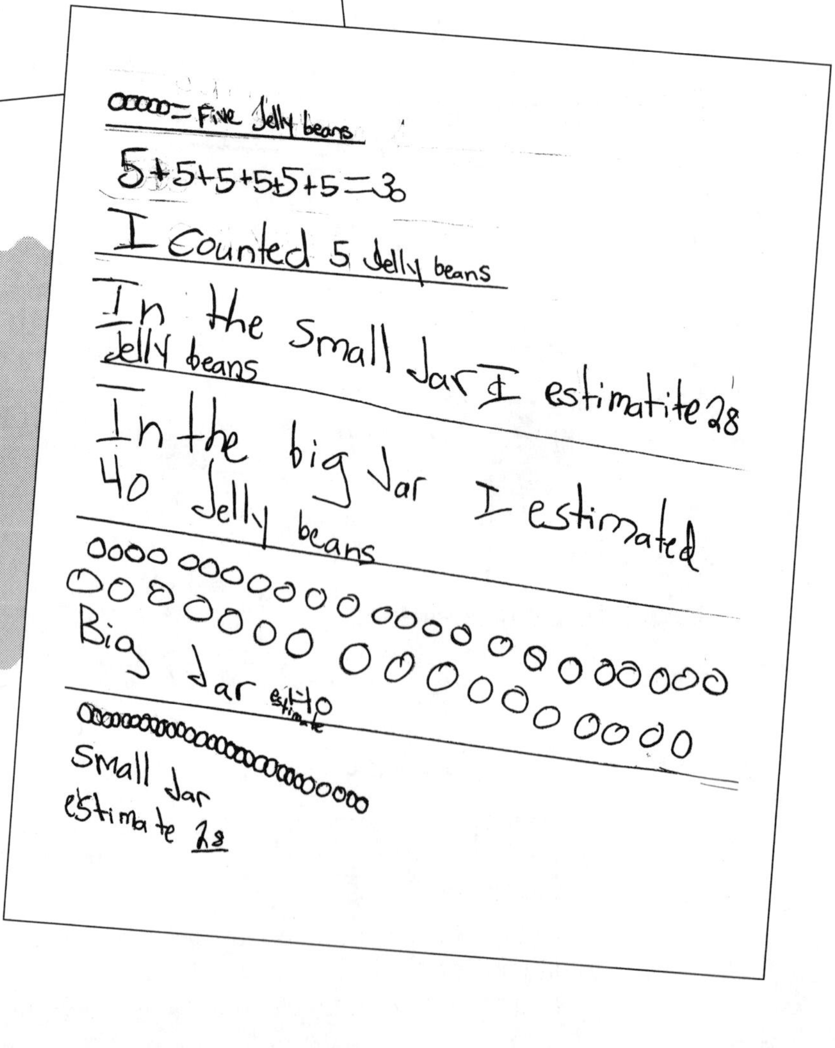


### Level 1 Response

This student uses two problem-solving strategies: counting and estimating. The strategies are explained very simply using words and symbols.

INVESTIGATION 2

# Packing Cookies

**Focus: Number Sense and Numeration**

In this investigation, students are asked to show all the ways to arrange 24 cookies. To do this, students must develop different arrays for 24 in order to determine the size and shape of the necessary box.

## Curriculum Expectations

- Understand and explain basic operations involving whole numbers by modelling and discussing a variety of problem situations.
- Develop proficiency in multiplying and dividing one-digit whole numbers.
- Solve problems and describe and explain the variety of strategies used.
- Justify in oral or written expression the method chosen for addition and subtraction; include reference to estimation, mental computation, concrete materials, or calculators.
- Interpret multiplication and division sentences in a variety of ways.
- Use appropriate strategies to solve number problems involving whole numbers.

## Prior Knowledge/Skills

Students should have some experience with:

- adding and multiplying;
- problem solving;
- strategizing to arrive at a number of different solutions;
- using arrays; and
- explaining their thinking.

## Materials

blank paper
pencils
manipulatives such as 24 colour tiles
grid paper (Make this available, but do not hand it out.)

## Grouping Arrangement

Introduce the problem in a large group. Students will work individually on the task.

## Presenting the Problem

1. To make this problem concrete, place a tub of 30 colour tiles on a table. Ask students how the tiles could be organized. Discuss and display one sample answer.
2. Put the investigation on the overhead and read it aloud with students. Discuss what is in the picture and what is being asked. Point out that there are many ways to organize 24 cookies.

3. Tell the students to develop as many different ways as they can.
4. Review the assessment criteria with students. Make sure that they understand what you are looking for in an answer.

### Assessment Criteria

It is important to let students know what will be evaluated before they start their task.

Tell them that you are interested in finding out:

- how many different ways they can organize the cookies;
- what packing strategies they use;
- how clearly they communicate their strategies; and
- what each different box would look like.

### Prompts for Getting Started

Some students initially may have difficulty getting started in their thinking. Others may feel that they are done after having presented one way to package 24 cookies. Some prompts to help them continue in their investigation include:

- What are you being asked to do? What is a good way to begin?
- How can you organize 24 cookies?
- What manipulatives might you use to help you?
- Is there another box design you could use?
- What strategies might help you do this problem?
- Is your plan clear and easy to understand?

## Assessing the Work

Assessment of this investigation should focus on the different arrays for showing 24; e.g., $24 \times 1$, $12 \times 2$, etc. Evaluate the clarity and thoroughness of student communication of each array and box size and type. Note whether students consider how each array might affect the box used. Some students will develop only one or two simple arrays and box types. Others may develop several. Still others may develop a combination of simple and more complex arrays and box types. Consider the complexity of the arrays used and how students use the arrays to determine box sizes and types.

### Hints for Scoring a Response

Student responses are being assessed for the level of mathematical understanding they represent. As you assess each response, consider the following questions:

- Did the student need assistance to get started?
- Did the student need assistance to complete the task?
- How well did the student demonstrate an ability to create a variety of ways to show 24 (i.e., using multiplication and division)?
- Are the boxes appropriate for each array?
- Is there more than one array and box type?
- How complex is each array and box type?
- How well organized and innovative are the packaging methods?

## Scoring Rubric

See page 24.

## Consolidating Learning

1. At the end of the activity, have students share some of their arrays. Discuss the difference in the arrays and box types. Also, discuss the difference in the arrays and how each affects the box type.
2. After the above discussion, work as a class to list the things students might consider when planning box types.
3. Challenge students to use this discussion to improve the level of their response.

## Follow-Up Activity

1. Test some of the student plans by having a class or school bake sale. Try a variety of ways to organize or package items.
2. Have students use multiplication or the repeat key on a calculator to calculate the total number of cookies represented by:
   - their own response;
   - the responses in their group; and
   - the responses in the entire class.

Investigation 2

# Packing Cookies Rubric

Name________________________ Date____________

| Expectations | Level 1 | Level 2 | Level 3 | Level 4 |
|---|---|---|---|---|
| **Problem Solving**<br><br>3m8 | With assistance, begins to develop a plan for organizing 24 cookies. | With some assistance, begins to develop a few ways to organize 24 cookies. | Devises a variety of ways to organize 24 cookies. | Devises a variety of simple and complex ways to organize 24 cookies. |
| **Understanding of Concepts**<br><br>3m4 | Demonstrates a limited understanding. Needs assistance to consider how the array chosen explains the basic operation of ÷ or x. | Demonstrates some understanding. Needs some assistance to consider how the arrays chosen explain basic operations of ÷ and x. | Considers different ways to organize and box 24 cookies. Shows some understanding of how the arrays chosen explain basic operations of ÷ and x. | Considers different and innovative ways to organize and box 24 cookies. Shows a clear understanding of how the arrays chosen explain basic operations of ÷ and x. |
| **Application of Procedures**<br><br>3m6, 3m23 | Needs assistance in using ÷ and x to develop different arrays for 24; work includes major errors or omissions. | Needs some assistance in using ÷ and x to develop different arrays for 24; work includes several minor errors or omissions. | Uses ÷ and x to produce several clear arrays for 24; work includes a few minor errors. | Produces a number of simple and complex arrays for 24 using ÷ and x; work may have a few very minor errors. |
| **Communication**<br><br>3m8 | With assistance, gives a limited explanation of the plan for organizing cookies. | With some assistance, gives some explanation of the plan for organizing cookies. | Gives a generally clear explanation of the plan for organizing cookies. | Gives a clear and creative explanation of the plan for organizing cookies. |

• See CD-ROM for additional regional rubrics.

Comments:

### Level 4 Response

This student devises a variety of ways to organize 24 cookies. For each, she considers a different way to box the cookies. The response shows complex arrays with very minor errors. Notice how well organized the solutions are and how each array shows both ÷ and x. Also notice how each array affects the box type and size.

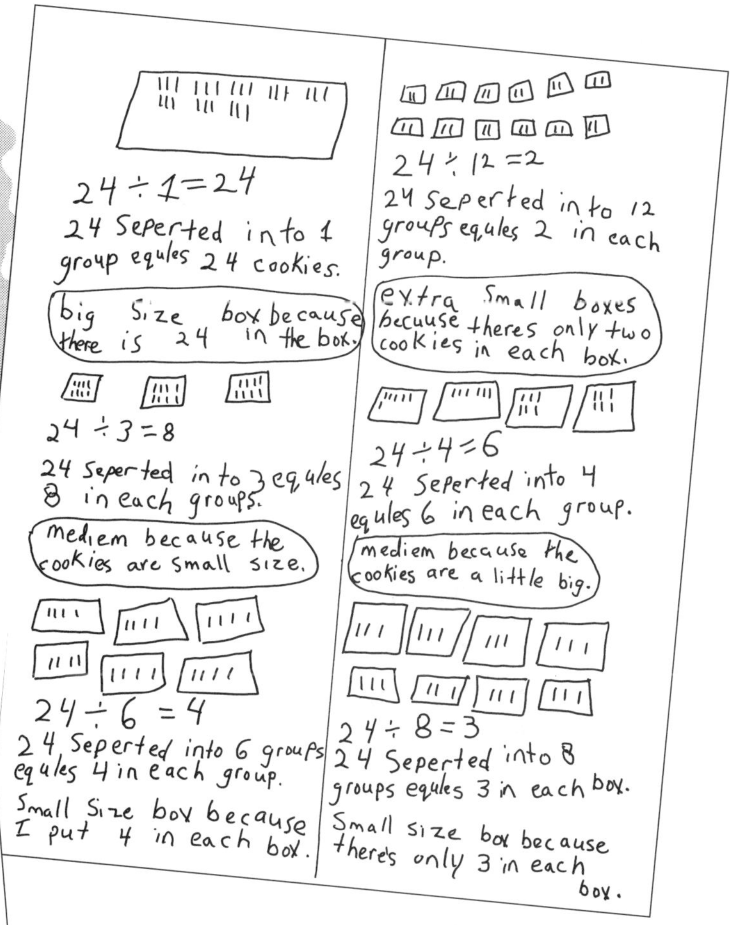
24 ÷ 1 = 24
24 Seperted into 1 group equles 24 cookies.
big Size box because there is 24 in the box.
24 ÷ 3 = 8
24 Seperted into 3 equles 8 in each groups.
mediem because the cookies are small size.
24 ÷ 6 = 4
24 Seperted into 6 groups equles 4 in each group.
Small Size box because I put 4 in each box.
24 ÷ 12 = 2
24 Seperted into 12 groups equles 2 in each group.
extra Small boxes becuuse theres only two cookies in each box.
24 ÷ 4 = 6
24 Seperted into 4 equles 6 in each group.
mediem because the cookies are a little big.
24 ÷ 8 = 3
24 Seperted into 8 groups equles 3 in each box.
Small size box because there's only 3 in each box.

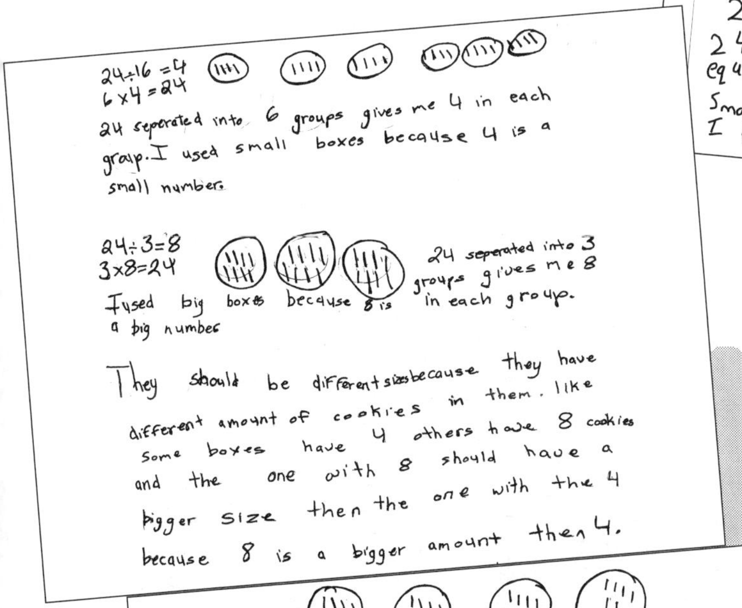
24÷6=4
6x4=24
24 seperated into 6 groups gives me 4 in each grup. I used small boxes because 4 is a small number.
24÷3=8
3x8=24
24 seperated into 3 groups gives me 8 in each group.
I used big boxes because 8 is a big number
They should be different sizes because they have different amount of cookies in them. like some boxes have 4 others have 8 cookies and the one with 8 should have a bigger size then the one with the 4 because 8 is a bigger amount then 4.

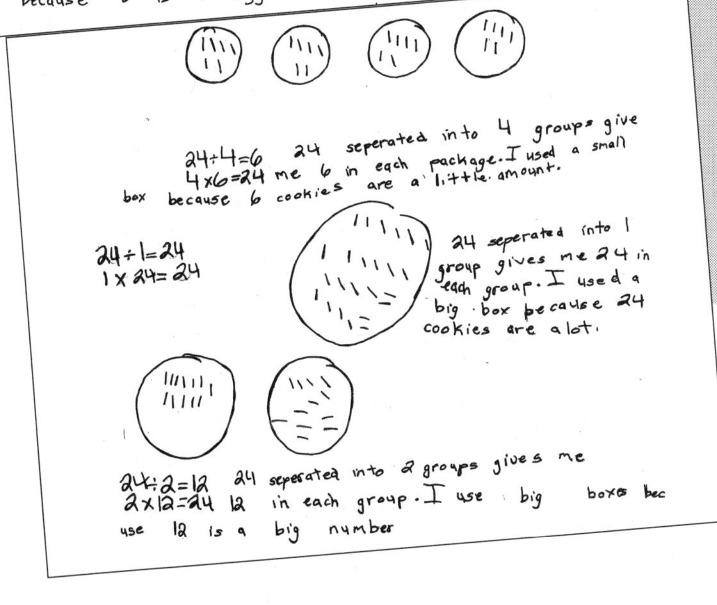
24÷4=6
4x6=24
24 seperated into 4 groups give me 6 in each package. I used a small box because 6 cookies are a little amount.
24÷1=24
1x24=24
24 seperated into 1 group gives me 24 in each group. I used a big box because 24 cookies are a lot.
24÷2=12
2x12=24
24 seperated into 2 groups gives me 12 in each group. I use big boxes bec use 12 is a big number

### Level 3 Response

This student shows a variety of ways to organize 24. The response uses both ÷ and x to communicate the arrays. There are several clear arrays. Each is clearly explained. The student communicates information about the box size for each array.

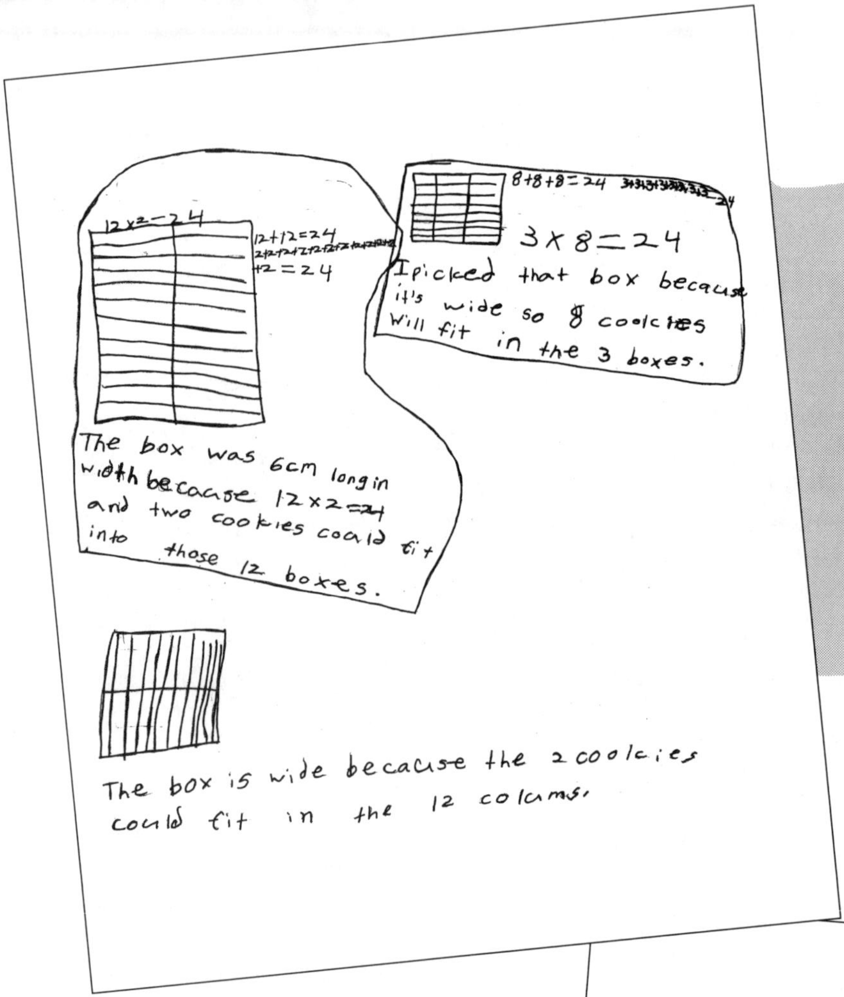


## Level 2 Response

This response provides the same basic solution communicated in two ways. The student uses addition to come up with the necessary arrays: 2 + 2 + 2 + 2 + 2 + 2 + 2 + 2 + 2 + 2 + 2 + 2 = 24. This is not extended into a multiplication sentence.

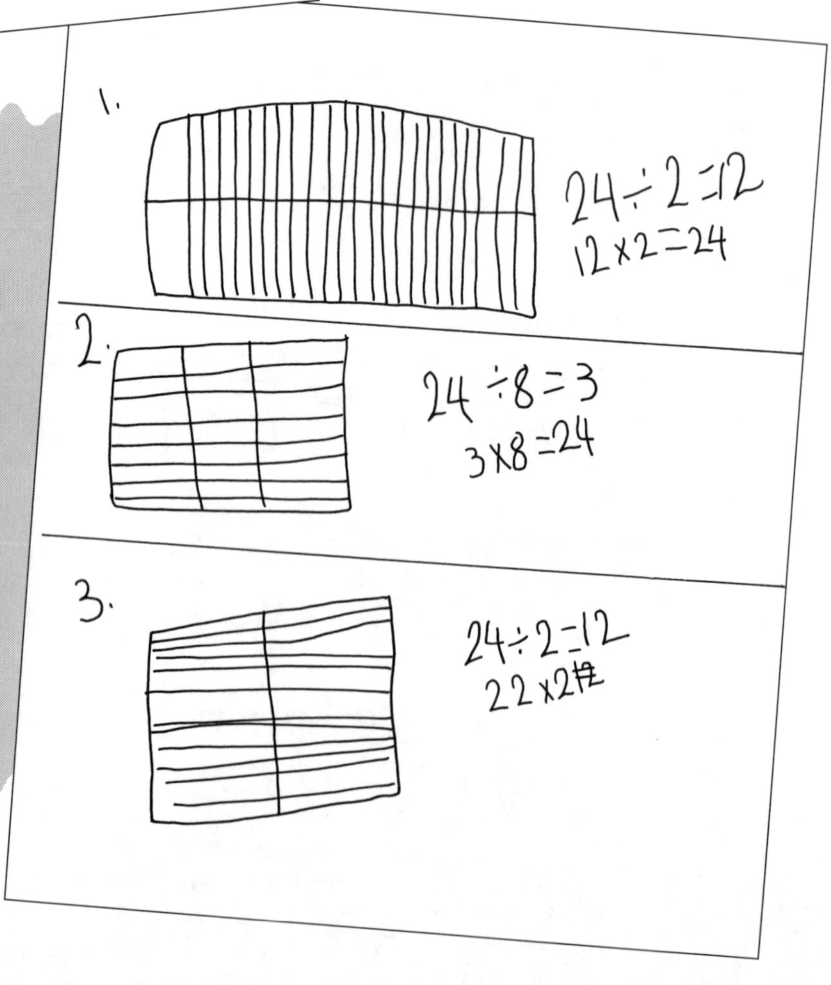


## Level 1 Response

This student has begun to develop some plans for organizing 24 cookies. The response shows two arrays for 24. The first and third examples list the same division. The first example shows an incorrect array. The array on the third example is correct. The plans show some limited understanding, with errors. There is no indication of any box for any array.

INVESTIGATION 3

# Share With Friends

**Focus: Number Sense and Numeration**

The purpose of this task is to challenge students to divide three chocolate bars among four people. Usually, students would simply cut each chocolate bar into four. In this case, a distracter has been added. The bars are each cut lengthwise into five pieces. Students have to consider whether to deal with these cuts. They are asked to develop as many different ways as they can to share the bars. This challenges students to work with the concept of quarters. The cuts in the bars ask them to consider fifths. How will they deal with any perceived contradiction? This problem provides students with an opportunity to think inside the box by dividing the 15 illustrated pieces among four people, and to think outside the box by cutting the bars widthwise.

## Curriculum Expectations

- Understand and explain basic operations involving whole numbers, by modelling and discussing a variety of problem situations.
- Solve problems and describe and explain the variety of strategies used.
- Represent and explain common fractions, presented in real-life situations, as part of a whole, part of a set, and part of a measure using concrete materials and drawings.

## Prior Knowledge/Skills

Students should have worked with many types of fractions, preferably using manipulatives. They should have practised communicating with pictures, words, and numbers.

## Materials

blank paper
pencils
crayons
manipulatives

## Grouping Arrangement

Introduce the problem in a large group. Students will work individually on the task.

## Presenting the Problem

1. Ask students to share experiences they have had sharing things with friends. Discuss fairness using the different things they have shared in the past. Make the discussion concrete by displaying two items (such as a piece of cake and a length of licorice) you wish to divide among three students. Ask students how to divide the items fairly. Discuss the various ways.
2. Display the question on the overhead. Read it aloud. Have students clarify each part of the picture and the number of each item. Discuss what is being asked.
3. When students are sure what to do, remind them to show all the ways they can think of to share the chocolate bars. Ask them to explain their thinking. Encourage them to use manipulatives. They can use pictures, words, and numbers to report.
4. Review the assessment criteria with the students. Make sure that they understand what you will look for in an answer.

### Assessment Criteria

It is important to let students know what will be evaluated before they start their task. Tell them that you are interested in finding out:

- how many ways they can share the bars fairly;
- whether their sharing is actually fair (they might provide reasons if the portions are not equal); and
- how clearly they can communicate what they have done.

### Prompts for Getting Started

Some students initially may have difficulty getting started in their thinking. Others may feel that they are done after having presented only one way to divide the bars or after dividing the bars into unequal portions, without any explanation. Some prompts to help them continue in their investigation include:

- What things do you see in the picture to share with the people?
- How many people are sharing?
- Is there any other way the bars could be shared fairly?
- Can you explain how you shared the bars?
- Is this portion fair? (Pointing to one that isn't.) Can you make this portion fair? Can you provide a reason why it's okay for this portion to be unfair?

## Assessing the Work

Students should suggest more than one way of sharing the bars fairly. Some may suggest breaking the bars along the lines shown. They can then give each person three pieces. They might divide two of the remaining pieces into halves, and give each person one, and divide the final into quarters, giving each person one. Others may divide the remaining pieces differently or simply cut the bars along different lines than are shown in the illustration. When assessing student responses, look for evidence of division, fractions (i.e., quarters), and equality. Also look for an effort to explain their thinking.

### Hints for Scoring a Response

Student responses are being assessed for the level of mathematical understanding they represent. As you assess each response, consider the following questions:

- Did the student need assistance to get started?
- Did the student need assistance to complete the task?
- Did the student share all the bars fairly? How equal are the portions?
- Did the student have a reason for providing any unequal portions?
- Did the student show different ways to share the bars?
- How complex are the divisions?
- Did the student clearly explain the thinking involved?
- Did the student use the fraction ($\frac{1}{4}$)?

## Scoring Rubric

See page 30.

## Consolidating Learning

1. At the end of the activity period, share some of the higher-level responses with the class and have students explain what makes these level 3 and 4.
2. Have students look back at their own work and identify what qualities it shares with the level 3 and 4 samples. What qualities might be improved?
3. Challenge students to make changes they think would improve their original work.

## Follow-Up Activity

1. In pairs, have students suggest other groups of items they could share with a group of three to five friends. Have them draw the items and repeat the task using the new ideas they have come up with. Encourage them to use manipulatives to check the fairness of their divisions.
2. Have pairs share with the class the work they have completed. Ask the class to comment on whether the sharing is fair.
3. To emphasize the idea of an unfair division, you might want to show a group of items. Get three students to come to the front. Use manipulatives to show an unfair division of the items and give each student a share. Then, ask the class if the sharing is fair. After some discussion, ask how to change the sharing to make it fair.

INVESTIGATION 3

# Share With Friends Rubric

Name______________________________ Date____________

| Expectations | Level 1 | Level 2 | Level 3 | Level 4 |
|---|---|---|---|---|
| **Problem Solving**<br><br>3m8 | With assistance, demonstrates a limited understanding of the problem by dividing the bars. | With some assistance, demonstrates some understanding of the problem by dividing the bars fairly without considering the remainder. | Demonstrates a general understanding by independently dividing the bars fairly; attempts to handle the remainder; may provide more than one solution. | Demonstrates a thorough understanding by dividing the bars fairly and in multiple ways; provides ways of dealing with any remainder. |
| **Understanding of Concepts**<br><br>3m20 | Demonstrates a limited understanding of fractions by representing division(s) into four unequal portions without considering the remainder. | Demonstrates some understanding of fractions by representing division(s) into four equal portions without considering the remainder. | Demonstrates general understanding of fractions by representing division(s) into four equal portions; provides an unequal way of dividing the remainder. | Demonstrates a thorough understanding of fractions by representing division(s) into four equal portions; equally divides any remainder. |
| **Application of Procedures**<br><br>3m4 | Divides the bars into portions. | Divides the bars into four portions. | Divides the bars into four equal portions; may divide any remainder into unequal portions. | Divides the bars, including any remainder, into four equal portions. |
| **Communication**<br><br>3m8 | Gives a limited explanation of division, fractions, or fairness. | Gives some explanation of fair division. | Gives a generally clear explanation of the equal and fair division of a whole. | Gives a clear and precise explanation of fair division. |

• See CD-ROM for additional regional rubrics.

Comments:

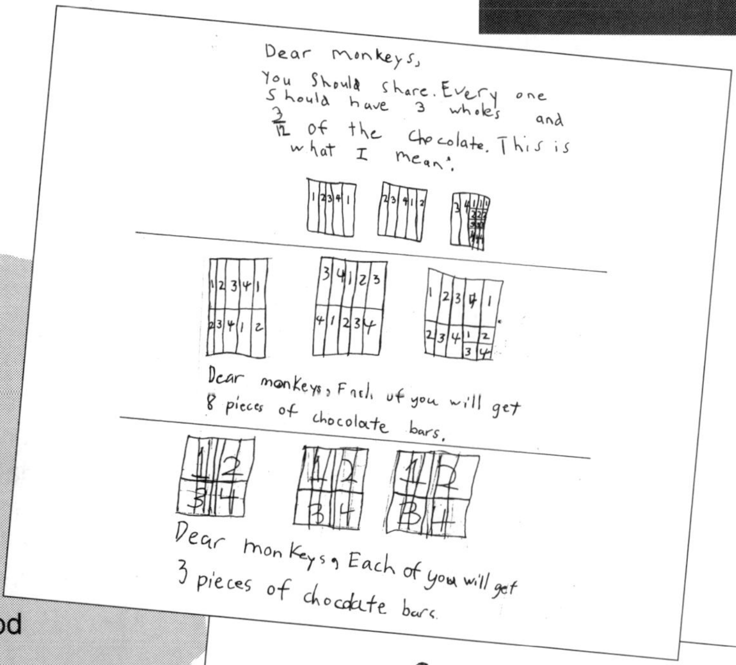


## Level 4 Response

This student suggests several ways of fairly sharing the chocolate bars. Sometimes, the student uses different portions as the units, demonstrating a clear understanding of the nature of fractions as parts of a whole. Notice the good organization and use of "Dear Monkeys" to explain how the bars will be divided. This response is thorough and clearly communicated.

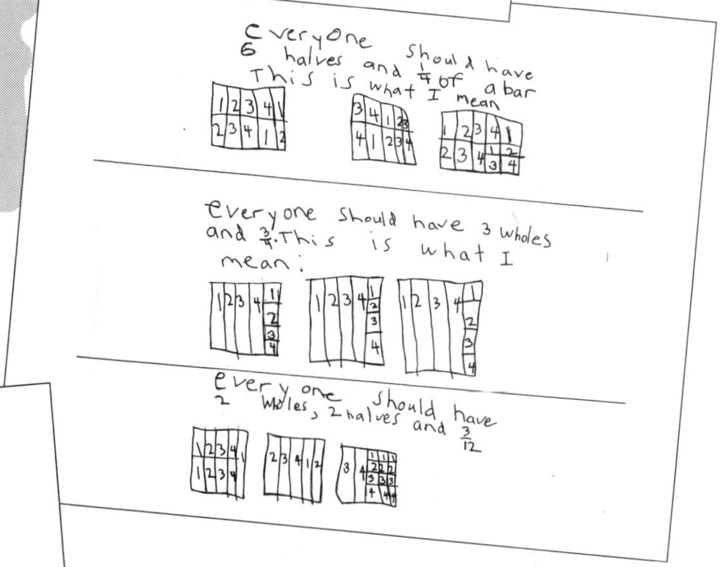


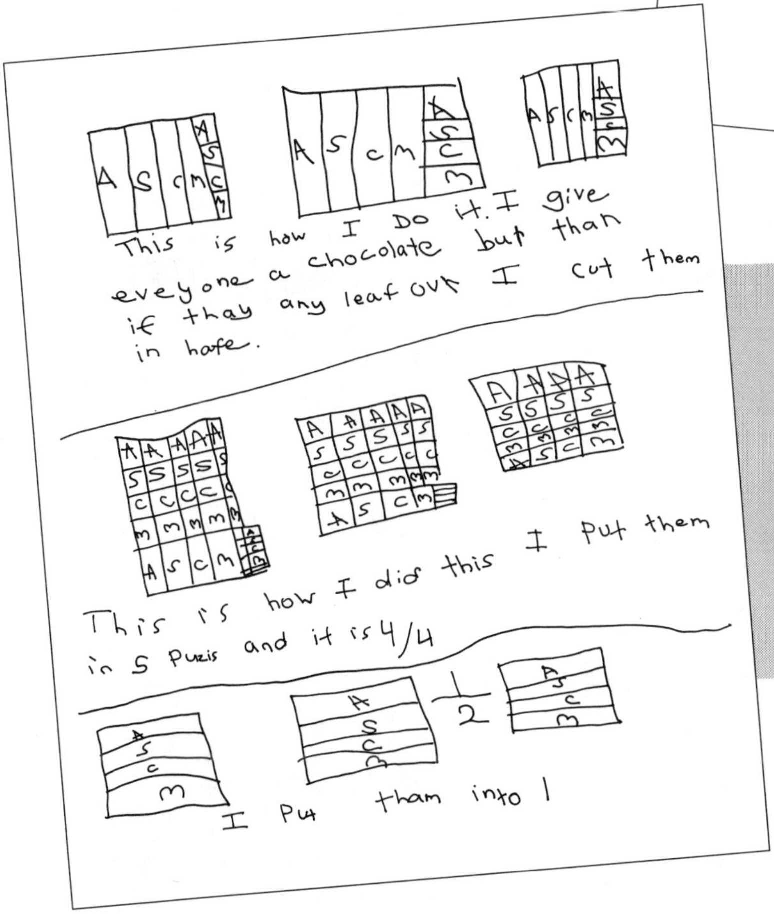


## Level 3 Response

This response provides some solutions. Each solution is shown with clear pictures and visual references to fractions. Some numerical terms for fractions are also used. The response is organized.

## Level 2 Response

This response demonstrates some understanding of sharing fairly between friends. Two ideas for sharing are provided. Each idea is partially correct. The student uses some terms for fractions, but uses them incorrectly. The communication is somewhat clear.

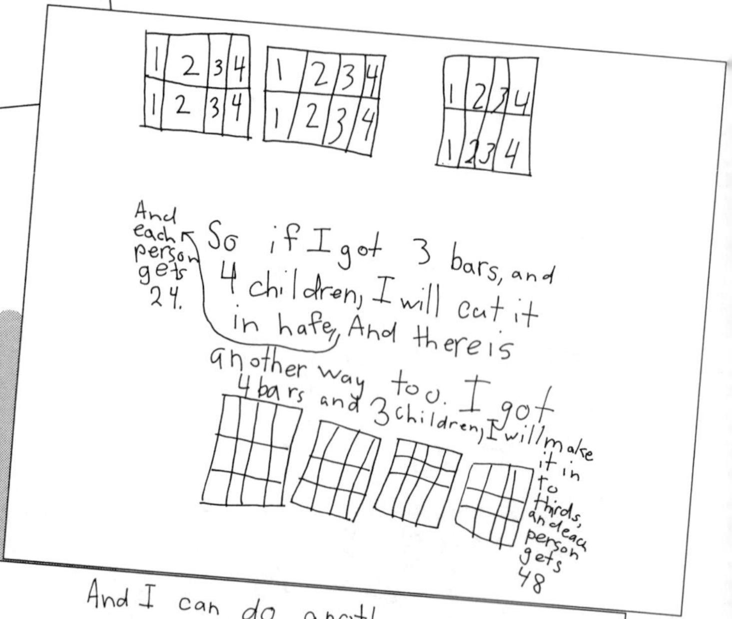

## Level 1 Response

This response demonstrates a limited understanding of the division. One response is partially correct. The divisions of the bar do not consider the divisions currently on the bars. The verbal response suggests that the student does not understand the divisions suggested by the pictures; i.e., that the bars need to be shared evenly by four children, and that the bars are currently divided into fifths.

# Measure a Friend

**Focus: Measurement**

In this investigation, students are challenged to find ways of measuring a snowman. They are provided with the opportunity to demonstrate that they understand different attributes of measurement and are familiar with some standard and non-standard units of measurement. This problem provides students with the opportunity to show what they know in a problem-solving context.

## Curriculum Expectations

- Demonstrate an understanding of and ability to apply measurement terms such as centimetre, metre, kilometre; millilitre, litre; gram, kilogram; degree Celsius; and week, month, year.
- Solve problems related to their day-to-day environment using measurement and estimation.
- Estimate, measure, record and compare the perimeter and the area of two-dimensional shapes.
- Estimate, measure, record, and compare the capacity of containers and the mass of familiar objects.
- Select the most appropriate unit of measure to measure length.
- Estimate, measure, and record linear dimensions of objects.
- Compare and order objects by their linear dimensions.
- Measure and compare the perimeter of two-dimensional shapes using standard units.
- Estimate, measure, and compare the area of shapes using uniform non-standard units; order the shapes by area.
- Estimate, measure, record, and compare the capacity of containers using standard units.
- Estimate, measure, and record the mass of familiar objects using standard units.

## Prior Knowledge/Skills

Students will have been exposed to a variety of measuring experiences. They should have prior opportunities to investigate:

- linear measurements for length, width, height, perimeter, and circumference in standard and non-standard units;
- area measurements in standard and non-standard units; and
- attributes such as mass, volume, and temperature.

Prior to trying this activity, provide students with oral and written opportunities to communicate directions.

## Materials

blank paper
pencils and crayons
measuring tools, including a variety of counters

## Grouping Arrangement

Introduce the problem in a large group. Students will work individually on the task.

# Presenting the Problem

1. If it is possible, build a snowman prior to doing the activity! If available, read the class a story such as *Sadie and the Snowman* (by Allen Morgan). This lovely story tells of a girl who builds a snowman and then rebuilds it throughout the winter as the sun melts the snow and as animals eat the eyes, nose, and mouth. It provides an excellent launch for the measurement question.
2. Tell the students that they are going to do a question that will let them show what they know about measurement.
3. Read the problem to the class. Describe the picture to them, clarifying that they must think of different ways to measure the snowman.
4. Clarify that their job is to write how to measure the snowman. Clarify that the picture in this problem shows a real thing.
5. Remind students that they should describe how to measure as many attributes as they can. They can use pictures, words, and numbers to show their ideas.
6. Review the assessment criteria with the students.

## Assessment Criteria

It is important to review with students how they will be assessed. In considering the Measure a Friend problem, students should be aware that they could:

- measure different attributes of the snowman (i.e., length, width, etc.);
- use different measuring tools;
- use different units of measurement;
- communicate their ideas in any way that best shows what they mean; and
- use words, numbers, and pictures as effective ways of communicating.

## Prompts for Getting Started

Some students initially may have difficulty getting started in their thinking. Others may feel that they are done after having presented only one type of measurement. The following prompts may help students continue in their investigation:

- What do you see in the picture? What are you trying to measure? (Clarify that they understand the question.)

- Pretend that you are on the telephone telling your friend about the snowman. What might you say about the snowman's size and how to measure it?
- How might your friend do this? What other ideas might the friend have?
- Explain to me, orally, how you might measure this snowman. (Listen to the oral explanation, encourage further detail, and then challenge the student to put on paper exactly what was just said.)

## Assessing the Work

In this assessment, look for what students know about different attributes, different measuring tools, and different units. They can suggest measuring width, length, height, perimeter, mass, volume, and surface area. They may refer to the snowman's age (it looks pretty fresh), mass, and temperature; suggest melting the snowman to get some idea of its volume; or suggest comparing the snowman to other objects. They may choose to discuss measuring in standard units or non-standard units. They may consider various aspects of the snowman, such as the hat, mitts, scarf, cane, nose, eyes, mouth, and buttons.

### Hints for Scoring a Response

Student responses are being assessed for the level of mathematical understanding they represent. As you assess each response, consider the following questions:

- Did the student need assistance to get started?
- Did the student need assistance to complete the task?
- What measurement strategies did the student suggest using?
- How well did the student explain each strategy?
- How many attributes did the student suggest measuring?
- What aspects of measurement did the student suggest using?
- What measurement terms did the student use?
- What measurement units did the student use? How effectively was each used?

## Scoring Rubric

See page 37.

## Consolidating Learning

1. Provide students with the opportunity to "show and tell" their work to the other students. Allow all students a chance to show one of their methods.
2. As a student is showing one solution, ask the rest of the group: "How many of you measured this attribute?"
3. As the students explain each measurement attribute, identify the attribute for the rest of the class. If the class has a "word wall" or if students use personal dictionaries, post or record new attributes

there. This works exceptionally well if the student who suggested the new attribute is acknowledged. For example, you might post: "Patricia chose to measure the temperature."

## Follow-Up Activities

1. Compare other objects to a snowman. Find an object that is bigger in some ways but smaller in other ways. Explain.
2. Provide students with building opportunities. Have students hide their building and use measurement terms to describe it orally (and later in writing) to a partner. The partner must then try to create the same structure based on the description.

INVESTIGATION 4

# Measure a Friend Rubric

Name_______________________________ Date____________

| Expectations | Level 1 | Level 2 | Level 3 | Level 4 |
|---|---|---|---|---|
| **Problem Solving**<br><br>3m34, 3m36, 3m40, 3m51, 3m52, 3m53 | Demonstrates a very limited understanding of how to measure by choosing a few simple strategies. | Demonstrates limited understanding of how to measure by choosing some appropriate strategies. | Demonstrates a general understanding by choosing and using appropriate measurement strategies. | Demonstrates a thorough understanding by selecting standard and non-standard measurement methods. |
| **Understanding of Concepts**<br><br>3m34, 3m37, 3m40, 3m41, 3m51, 3m52, 3m54 | Demonstrates a very limited understanding of measurement concepts (e.g., length, width, area, mass, temperature). | Demonstrates some understanding of measurement concepts (e.g., length, width, area, mass, temperature). | Demonstrates a clear understanding of measurement concepts (e.g., length, width, area, mass, temperature). | Demonstrates a thorough understanding of measurement concepts (e.g., length, width, area, mass, temperature). |
| **Application of Procedures**<br><br>3m34, 3m38, 3m40, 3m41 | Represents measurement of only 1 attribute. Suggests using limited number of measurement tools or using them inappropriately. | Represents measurement of a few attributes. Suggests using some measurement tools, somewhat appropriately. | Represents measurement of most attributes. Suggests using a variety of tools appropriately. | Represents measurement of many attributes, and possibly more than one way to measure an attribute (e.g., standard and non-standard units). Suggests using a variety of tools creatively. |
| **Communication**<br><br>3m34, 3m37, 3m40, 3m42 | Uses some pictures and a few measurement terms to describe the process. | Uses pictures and some correct measurement terminology to describe the process. | Uses pictures and correct terms (e.g., length, width, perimeter, area, temperature) to describe the process. | Uses pictures and appropriate terms (e.g., length, width, age, perimeter, area, mass, temperature) to describe the process. |

• See CD-ROM for additional regional rubrics.

Comments:

### Level 4 Response

This student has provided words, visuals, and clear formatting to provide a thorough explanation of many ways to measure the snowman. Quite a variety of attributes are mentioned: height, width, volume, mass, and circumference. Each method includes a visual that clearly shows how the attribute can be measured. Both standard and non-standard measuring tools are referred to. A variety of standard measurement terms are used.

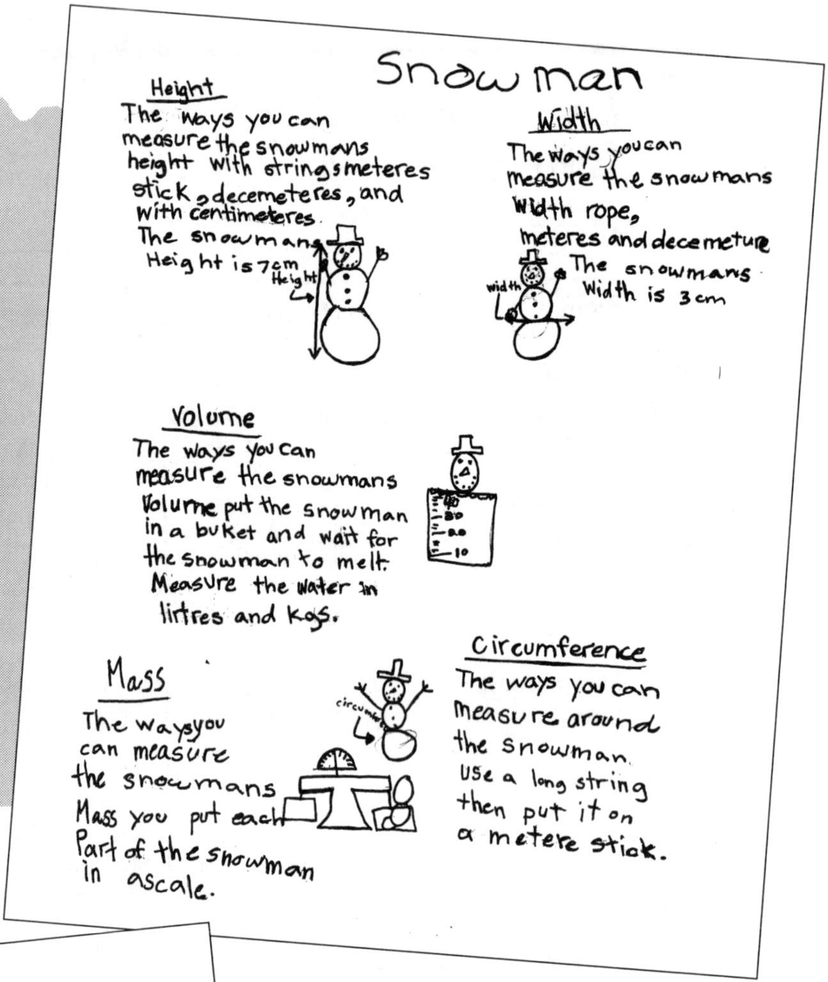

### Level 3 Response

This is another high level response that uses appropriate terms. The student has provided words and clear visuals to communicate how to measure height, width, mass, and volume. Both standard and non-standard measurement tools are referred to, and the student follows through with an explanation of how to use each. Clear measurement terms are used. The student has some idea of mass, but is not clear on how it should be measured.

I can use a meter stick to measure the Snowman's height I can also use measuring tape to see how many he is. and I can use a strings to see how many cm he is. He he is 7cm tall.
circumference I can use string to see it's circumference I can also use measureing tape to see how many cm. or m. the Snow man is. he is four cm wide.

**Level 2 Response**

This student discusses two aspects of measurement: height and circumference. The response displays good if limited thinking. A number of tools and units are mentioned. The student explores a limited number of methods for measuring the snowman.

**Level 1 Response**

This student concentrates on measuring one attribute of the snowman. The tools and terms are appropriate for this one attribute. Standard measurement terms are used correctly. The student explores a very limited number of methods for measuring the snowman.

I can use Tapmeasure, metre Stick,
The Sonw man 11 cm.
hight
the sonw mans Botte is 15 cM.

INVESTIGATION 5

# What Can You Buy?

## Focus: Number Sense and Numeration/Measurement

In this investigation, students are challenged to come up with their own problems, and then to solve them. This role of problem writer puts some interesting demands on students as they must gather information from the visual, and then decide how to use this information to formulate problems. As part of this investigation, students need to review their problems to verify that the questions make sense in the context of the picture. Also, they need to make sure that the problems are clearly stated — and develop an answer for each one.

### Curriculum Expectations

- Solve problems and describe and explain the variety of strategies used.
- Add and subtract three-digit numbers with and without regrouping using concrete materials.
- Pose and solve number problems involving more than one operation.
- Use appropriate strategies to solve number problems involving whole numbers.
- Demonstrate the relationship between all coins and bills up to $100.
- Make purchases and change for money amounts up to $10; estimate, count, and record the value up to $10 of a collection of coins and bills.
- Read and write money amounts using two forms of notation (89¢ and $0.89).

### Prior Knowledge/Skills

Students need to know how to:

- add money amounts to $5; and
- add and subtract three-digit numbers with and without regrouping, possibly using concrete materials.

### Materials

blank paper
pencils
crayons
$2, $1, quarters, dimes, nickels, and pennies, or manipulatives that represent them

### Grouping Arrangement

Introduce the problem in a large group. Students will work individually on the task.

## Presenting the Problem

1. Make sure that students know what a word problem is. To help them, make up a word problem with them, or show them one they have recently solved. Point out that word problems have numbers and words — and usually end with a question.
2. Distribute the investigation and read it aloud with the students. Explain that the word problems they write should use information from the picture. Encourage them to consider that the role of teacher and student has changed. Here is their chance to create problems for someone else to solve. They can use symbols, words, and numbers.
3. Tell the students that they have to solve the problems they create. Later, students may be challenged to solve the problems another student wrote. For that reason, encourage students to make sure that their problems are clear enough for someone else to understand. They might check the clarity of their work by asking themselves:
   - What am I asking someone else to do?
4. Review the assessment criteria with students. Make sure they understand what you are looking for in an answer.

### Assessment Criteria

It is important to let students know what they will be evaluated on before they start their task. Tell them that you are interested in finding out:

- how many different kinds of problems they can write;
- whether their problems make sense; and
- to a lesser extent, whether they can solve their own problems.

### Prompts for Getting Started

Some students initially may have difficulty getting started in their thinking. Others may feel that they are done after having presented only one problem or one type of problem. The following prompts may help them to continue in their investigation:

- What is shown in the picture? What information is given about each item? How can you use this in a problem?
- What kinds of math problems might you develop using this information?
- Can you think of another kind of problem to write?
- Is there an especially interesting way you might use the items here in a problem?

## Assessing the Work

In this assessment, look for different ways that students represent word problems and assess the complexity of these problems. Also, notice how students solve simple problems involving counting and joining, and investigate number meanings. Three-digit addition and subtraction sentences to $5 can be created, with or without regrouping. Concrete materials may or may not be used. Number sentences can be presented with various combinations of pictures, words, and symbols. Responses may range in mathematical thinking: from one or a small number of addition sentences that add to less than 500, to several addition *and* subtraction sentences that total 500 — or close to that amount. Students may work with cents only, or use a combination of cents and decimal notation (e.g., 5 cents or $.05).

### Hints for Scoring a Response

Student responses are being assessed for the level of mathematical understanding they represent. As you assess each response, consider the following questions:

- Did the student need assistance to get started?
- Did the student need assistance to complete the task?
- How many different kinds of problems did the student list?
- How complex is each question mathematically?
- Do the problems make sense?
- Are the solutions correct?
- How much money does the student spend? How does the student show any balance?
- What mathematical terms and symbols are used?

## Scoring Rubric

See page 43.

## Consolidating Learning

1. When the students have finished their reports, display some high-level responses and have the students discuss why these warrant a level 4.
2. Have students review their own reports and indicate what they might do to raise their level.
3. As a class, list the various erasers one can buy for $5.

## Follow-Up Activity

1. Have students create their own store with items that are priced similar to those in the picture.
2. Have students work with a partner to shop at the store and spend $5. Each student should be able to represent various addition and subtraction sentences, with and without regrouping, to $5.
3. As students work, encourage them to discuss what they are doing and help each other as they go along.
4. Have them share what they have done by presenting their findings to the class.

INVESTIGATION 5

# What Can You Buy? Rubric

Name______________________________ Date__________

| Expectations | Level 1 | Level 2 | Level 3 | Level 4 |
|---|---|---|---|---|
| **Problem Solving**<br><br>3m8 | Uses a limited number of strategies (e.g., guessing), often incorrectly or inaccurately. | Uses more than one strategy, usually correctly. | Uses several strategies, with few errors. | Uses several strategies (e.g., patterning, guess and check, repeated addition or subtraction), appropriately. |
| **Understanding of Concepts**<br><br>3m48, 3m49 | Demonstrates a very limited understanding of representing the sum of $5. | Demonstrates some understanding of representing the sum of $5. | Demonstrates a general understanding of combining numbers or symbols in different ways to represent the sum of $5. | Demonstrates a thorough understanding of combining numbers or symbols in different ways to represent the sum of $5. |
| **Application of Procedures**<br><br>3m29, 3m31, 3m32 | Uses a few ways of showing + and – to $5. Calculates with minimal accuracy. | Uses some ways to show + and – to $5 *or* spends most of the money or too much but may not show or explain a balance or the amount overspent. Calculates somewhat correctly. | Uses several complex ways to show + and – to $5 *and* spends all of the money or shows a correct balance left. Calculates with minor errors. | Uses several complex ways to show + and – to $5; shows several correct ways of spending the entire amount; shows a balance where indicated. Calculates accurately or with very minor errors. |
| **Communication**<br><br>3m32, 3m50 | Provides an unclear explanation; uses incomplete math terms or symbols. | Provides some clarity in explanations; uses some mathematical terms and symbols. | Provides a clear and concise explanation; uses appropriate mathematical terms and symbols. | Uses a range of appropriate terms and symbols to provide a clear and precise explanation of the methods used. |

• See CD-ROM for additional regional rubrics.

Comments:

## Level 4 Response

This student uses several complex ways to show addition and subtraction involving five dollars. The response correctly shows the cost of two and three erasers of various types (e.g., two star erasers cost ninety cents; three moon erasers cost ninety cents; six dog erasers cost four dollars and fifty cents). The student uses one main strategy (e.g., repeated addition) accurately and precisely. Note the different ways he makes sure that the entire five dollars is spent. All addition and subtraction is done correctly. The student writes down the name and cost of erasers correctly and spends the entire amount or shows a balance. The items bought are organized in a precise way. Grade-appropriate terms are used. Both cent and dollar signs are correctly used.

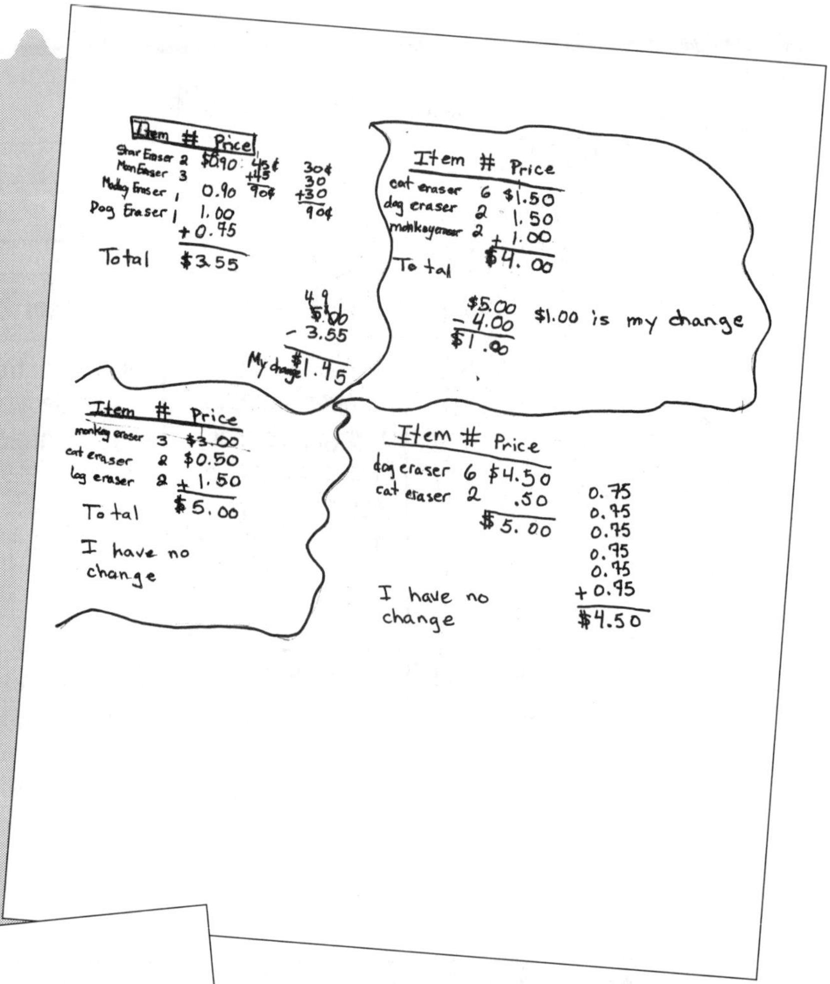

| Item | # | Price |
|---|---|---|
| Star Eraser | 2 | $0.90 |
| Moon Eraser | 3 | |
| Monkey Eraser | 1 | 0.90 |
| Dog Eraser | 1 | 1.00 |
| | | + 0.75 |
| Total | | $3.55 |

45¢ + 45 = 90¢; 30¢ + 30 + 30 = 90¢

$5.00 − 3.55 = My change $1.45

| Item | # | Price |
|---|---|---|
| cat eraser | 6 | $1.50 |
| dog eraser | 2 | 1.50 |
| monkey eraser | 2 | + 1.00 |
| To tal | | $4.00 |

$5.00 − 4.00 = $1.00   $1.00 is my change

| Item | # | Price |
|---|---|---|
| monkey eraser | 3 | $3.00 |
| cat eraser | 2 | $0.50 |
| dog eraser | 2 | + 1.50 |
| To tal | | $5.00 |

I have no change

| Item | # | Price |
|---|---|---|
| dog eraser | 6 | $4.50 |
| cat eraser | 2 | .50 |
| | | $5.00 |

0.75 + 0.75 + 0.75 + 0.75 + 0.75 + 0.75 = $4.50

I have no change

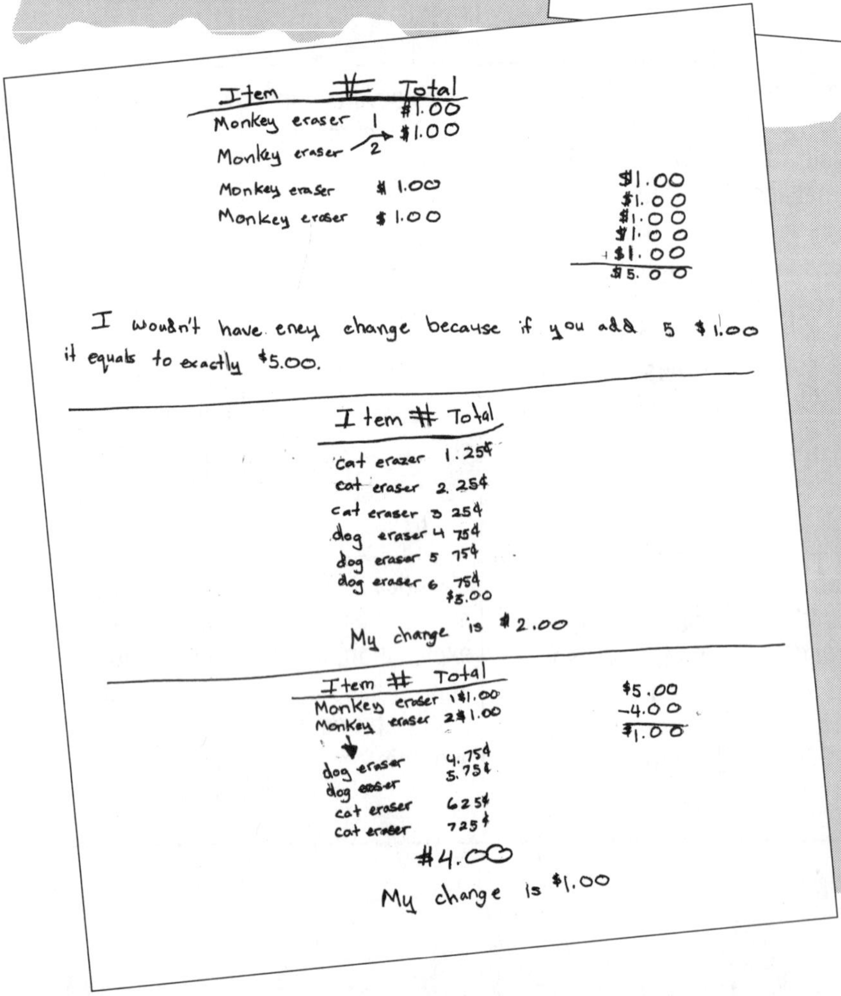

| Item | # | Total |
|---|---|---|
| Monkey eraser | 1 | $1.00 |
| Monkey eraser | 2 | $1.00 |
| Monkey eraser | | $1.00 |
| Monkey eraser | | $1.00 |

$1.00 + $1.00 + $1.00 + $1.00 + $1.00 = $5.00

I wouldn't have eney change because if you add 5 $1.00 it equals to exactly $5.00.

| Item | # | Total |
|---|---|---|
| cat erazer | 1 | 25¢ |
| cat eraser | 2 | 25¢ |
| cat eraser | 3 | 25¢ |
| dog eraser | 4 | 75¢ |
| dog eraser | 5 | 75¢ |
| dog eraser | 6 | 75¢ |
| | | $3.00 |

My change is $2.00

| Item | # | Total |
|---|---|---|
| Monkey eraser | 1 | $1.00 |
| Monkey eraser | 2 | $1.00 |
| dog eraser | | 4.75¢ |
| dog eraser | | 5.75¢ |
| cat eraser | | 625¢ |
| Cat eraser | | 725¢ |
| | | $4.00 |

$5.00 − 4.00 = $1.00

My change is $1.00

## Level 3 Response

This student uses several strategies to solve this problem. She demonstrates a general understanding of combining numbers and symbols to make five dollars. There are several complex ways of adding and subtracting to show a correct balance from five dollars. The setup provides a clear explanation of what was done, with minor errors. The response uses appropriate terms and symbols. Note the particularly interesting final example in which she correctly adds two monkey erasers, two dog erasers, and two cat erasers to make four dollars, with one dollar change, and her original efforts to find out how many monkey erasers she could purchase for five dollars.

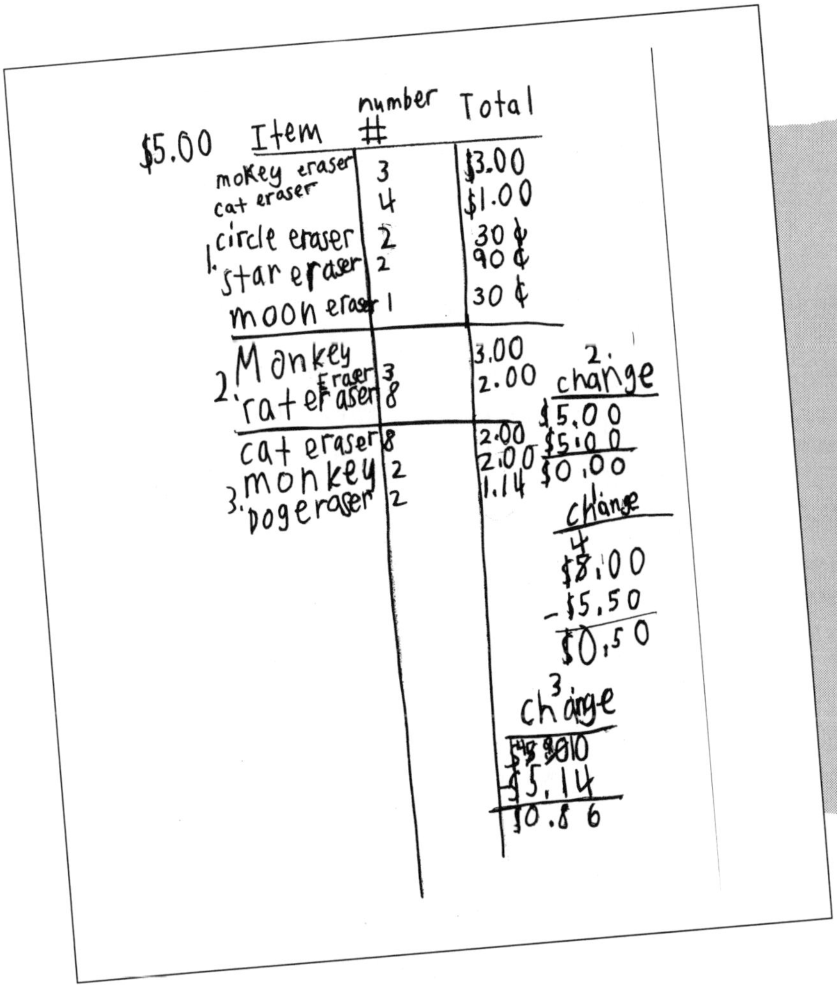


## Level 2 Response

This student shows some understanding of representing the sum of five dollars using addition and subtraction. The student clearly shows the items purchased and the number of each item. Note the second example, in which three monkey erasers and eight cat erasers total five dollars, with no change. It is not always clear how the sum for each item was calculated. A final total for each series is not always provided; there are several errors, including an incorrect setup for subtraction (i.e., the lower number is on top).

## Level 1 Response

This student uses one limited strategy, with major errors. The student writes down the eraser names correctly and correctly shows the amounts purchased. There is no indication of how the student calculated that two cat erasers cost one dollar and fifty cents. The addition question is properly set up, with a correct symbol. There is some evidence that the student is trying to carry. The addition itself is done inaccurately.

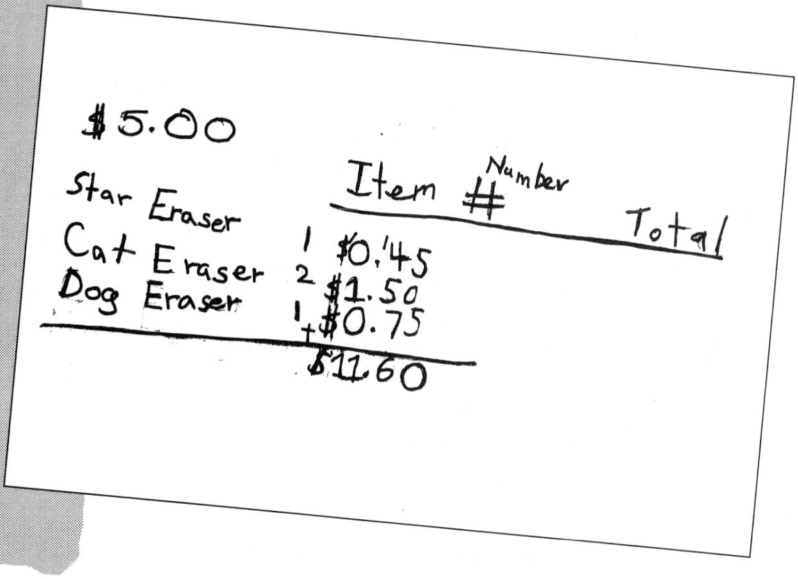

INVESTIGATION 6

# Sort Shapes

## Focus: Geometry and Spatial Sense

In this investigation, students are challenged to sort three-dimensional figures with various attributes. In order to sort these figures, they need to identify as many different attributes as they can, and then sort using these attributes. This investigation can be used to assess student understanding of three-dimensional figures and their many attributes.

### Curriculum Expectations

- Investigate the attributes of three-dimensional figures and two-dimensional shapes using concrete materials and drawings.
- Use language effectively to describe geometric concepts, reasoning, and investigations.
- Investigate the similarities and differences among a variety of prisms using concrete materials and drawings.
- Compare and sort two-dimensional shapes according to two or more attributes.
- Compare and sort three-dimensional figures according to two or more geometric attributes.
- Describe and name prisms and pyramids by the shape of their base.
- Explore and identify two-dimensional shapes using concrete materials and drawings.

### Prior Knowledge/Skills

Students need to know how to describe and identify figures, and identify the attributes of three-dimensional figures, including such things as the way circular and non-circular shapes might be used in these figures. They should have sorted shapes using concrete materials and drawings.

### Materials

blank paper
pencils
crayons
manipulatives of three-dimensional figures
visual from investigation enlarged (to use for a class sort)

### Grouping Arrangement

Introduce the problem in a large group. Students will work individually on the task.

## Presenting the Problem

1. Display an assortment of three-dimensional figures. Discuss with the class the attributes of these figures. Make a list of various attributes (e.g., size, combination of shapes).

2. Display the investigation on the overhead projector and read the question aloud for students. Discuss what the question means.
3. Display the large version of the set of figures and work with the class to develop one sample sort. Tape the sort on experience chart paper. Record the letters for this sort. Have students suggest a label for the sort. Discuss a possible sorting rule.
4. Remind students that this sort provides one idea. They can use it, but should develop other sorts. Point out that the question challenges them to sort the figures in many ways.
5. Encourage students to record the letters that show their sort, and use pictures, words, and symbols to explain the sorting rule.
6. Review the assessment criteria with students. Make sure that they understand what you are looking for in an answer.

### Assessment Criteria

It is important to let students know what will be evaluated before they start their task. Tell them that you are interested in finding out:

- how many different ways they can sort the figures;
- whether they use some mathematical attributes to sort figures;
- how well organized their sorts are;
- whether they can explain how each sort was done; and
- how well they explain sorting rules.

### Prompts for Getting Started

Some students initially may have difficulty getting started in their thinking. Others may feel that they are done after copying down the sample sort done by the class and possibly providing one other sort. Others may provide a number of sorts, but no sorting rules. Some prompts to help them continue in their investigation include:

- Can you think of another way to sort these figures?
- What other attribute might you use to sort these figures?
- Is there an especially interesting way you might sort these figures?
- How might you organize your sorts?
- What mathematical terms might you use to help you sort?
- What rule did you use to make this sort? How can you explain this in a sorting rule?

## Assessing the Work

This assessment focusses on how students describe, name, compare, and sort various three-dimensional figures. Note that students may include both mathematical and non-mathematical ways of sorting them. For example, they might sort the figures they like and the ones they don't like. This is fine. Push their thinking by asking what else the figures they like might have in common. Responses may range in mathematical thinking, demonstrating a very limited to a thorough understanding of figure attributes.

## Hints for Scoring a Response

Student responses are being assessed for the level of mathematical understanding they represent. As you assess each response, consider the following questions:

- Did the student need assistance to get started?
- Did the student need assistance to complete the task?
- How many different ways did the student use to sort the figures?
- How accurate were the sorts?
- How complex were the sorts?
- Do the sorts make sense?
- How well organized are the sorts?
- How well are the sorting rules communicated?

## Scoring Rubric

See page 49.

## Consolidating Learning

1. When the students have finished their reports, display some higher-level responses and have the students discuss why these warrant a level 4.
2. Have students review their own reports and indicate what they might do to raise them one level.
3. As a class, make and post a list of the various accurate and innovative solutions for sorting the figures.

## Follow-Up Activity

1. Have the students create their own problems using a variety of three-dimensional figures they make from assorted boxes, cylinders, and other “found” objects. Encourage them to use a variety of figures.
2. Then, they should ask a partner to sort these items in different ways and explain each sort. Students can do a manual sort, and then record what they did using pictures, words, and symbols.
3. Encourage students to discuss what they are doing and help each other as they work.
4. Have partners present one interesting sort to the class.

INVESTIGATION 6

# Sort Shapes Rubric

Name ______________________________ Date ______________

| Expectations | Level 1 | Level 2 | Level 3 | Level 4 |
|---|---|---|---|---|
| **Problem Solving**<br><br>3m55 | Demonstrates a very limited understanding of how to sort and explain shapes; provides an incomplete or inaccurate solution. | Demonstrates limited understanding of how to sort and explain shapes; provides a partially complete or accurate solution. | Demonstrates a general understanding of how to sort and explain shapes; provides complete and accurate solution(s). | Demonstrates a thorough understanding of how to sort and explain shapes; provides a number of complete, accurate, and innovative solutions. |
| **Understanding of Concepts**<br><br>3m61, 3m67 | Demonstrates a very limited understanding of comparing and sorting the shapes; uses few or no mathematical relationships. | Demonstrates limited understanding of comparing and sorting the shapes; uses some partially correct mathematical relationships. | Demonstrates general understanding of comparing and sorting the shapes; uses appropriate mathematical relationships. | Demonstrates a thorough understanding of comparing and sorting the shapes; uses appropriate and clear mathematical relationships. |
| **Application of Procedures**<br><br>3m65, 3m66 | Sorts a few shapes in a limited way. | Sorts some shapes in a limited way. | Sorts most shapes in several ways. | Sorts all shapes in a variety of ways. |
| **Communication**<br><br>3m60, 3m70 | Presentation and explanation of sorting rules are limited and unclear; rarely uses grade-appropriate vocabulary. | Presentation and explanation of sorting rules are somewhat evident; uses some grade-appropriate vocabulary. | Presentation and explanation of sorting rules are generally clear and somewhat precise; uses grade-appropriate vocabulary. | Presentation and explanation of sorting rules are clear and precise; frequently uses grade-appropriate vocabulary. |

• See CD-ROM for additional regional rubrics.

Comments:

### Level 4 Response

Notice the Venn diagram this student uses to report on one of her sorts. The Venn diagram shows how she has correctly sorted the shapes according to their number of vertices and edges. G, C, K, and J have eight vertices and 20 edges. I and A have three vertices and three edges. L and E have a hole and different numbers of vertices and edges. This is an extremely sophisticated sort presented in a sophisticated fashion. She has also reported on the shapes that have no vertices or edges: H, B, F, D. The response shows good communication and a high level of mathematical understanding.

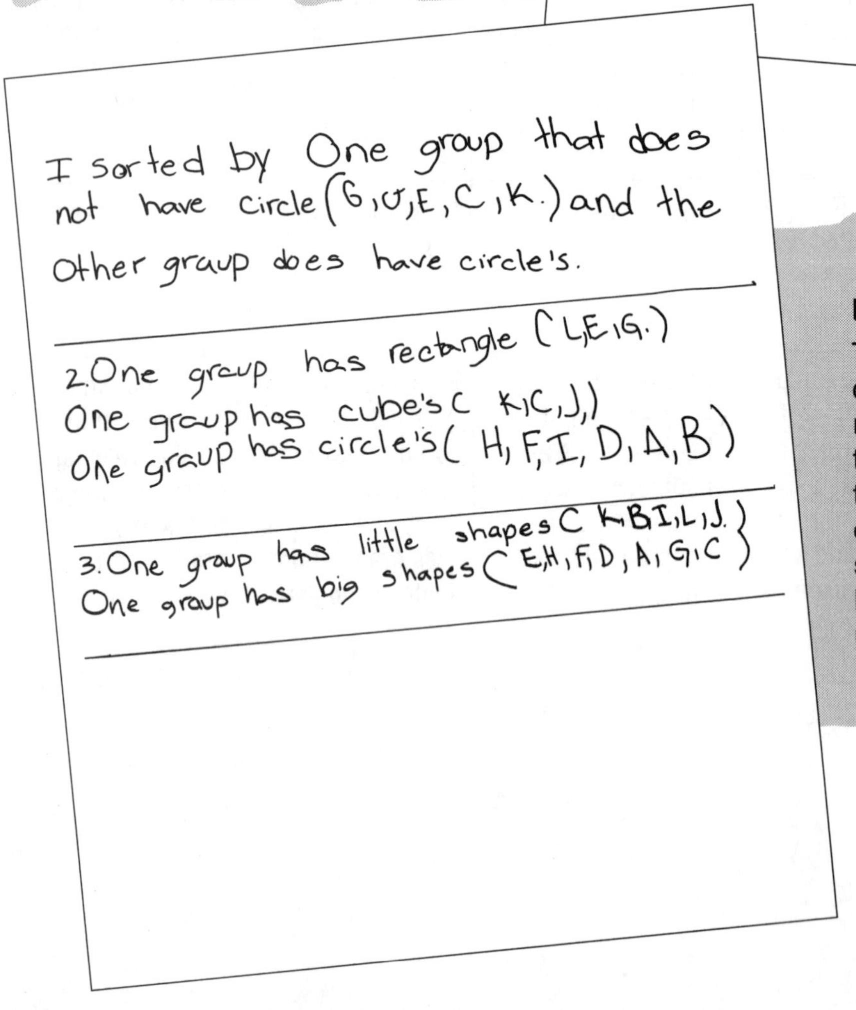


### Level 3 Response

This student has provided three clear, simple, and correct sorts. The response separates out the shapes that do not have a circle; identifies the shapes that have rectangles, cubes, and circles; and classifies the shapes according to size. Mathematical terminology is correctly used.

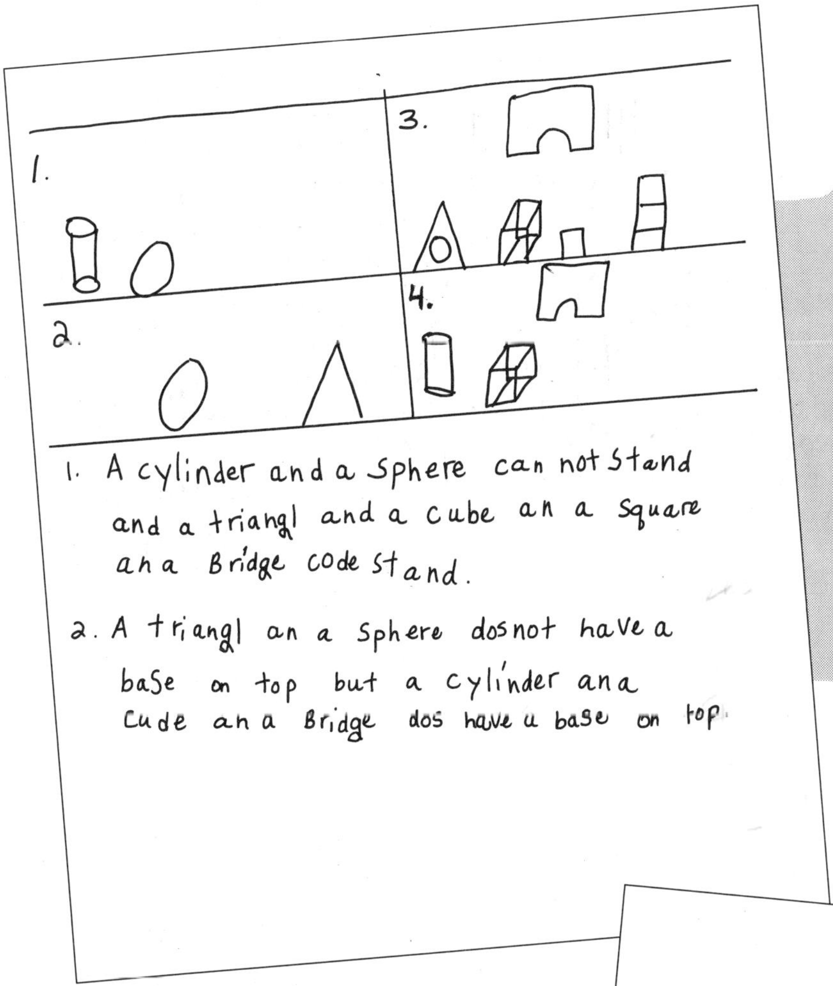


### Level 2 Response

This student has attempted to do two sorts. The first provides an interesting effort at differentiating shapes according to how they transform. The effort is inaccurately done. The second sort is simple and correct. The response shows some limited mathematical understanding.

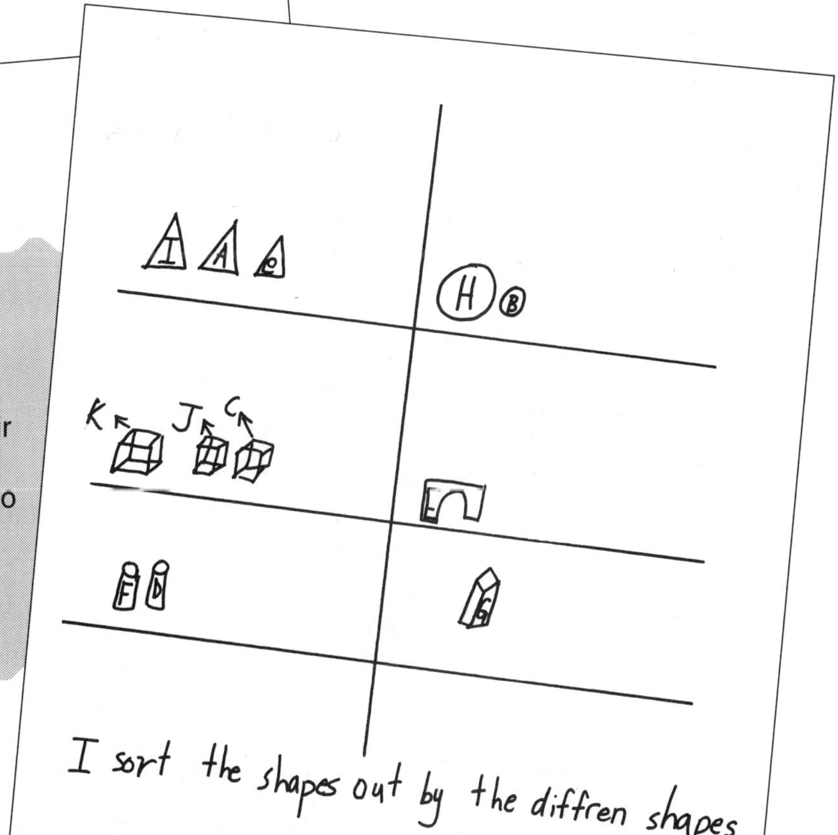


### Level 1 Response

This student has provided one sort that classifies A–L according to their different shapes. What is done is correct. It is very simple. There is no explanation. The shapes are not labelled.

INVESTIGATION 7

# Shape Game

**Focus: Geometry and Spatial Sense**

In this investigation, students are challenged to demonstrate their understanding of performing and describing transformations such as flips, slides, and turns (reflections, translations, and rotations). Students are expected to transform the shape in the upper left in various ways as they move it through the other three sections of the grid. Then, they are asked to explain each transformation and describe its location or movement on the grid.

### Curriculum Expectations

- Explore transformations of geometric figures.
- Describe location and movements on a grid.
- Use language effectively to describe geometric concepts, reasoning, and investigations.
- Identify transformations, such as flips, slides, and turns (reflections, translations, and rotations), using concrete materials and drawings.
- Perform rotations using concrete materials.
- Describe how to get from one point to another on a grid.

### Prior Knowledge/Skills

Before doing this activity, students should:

- have experience flipping, sliding, and turning concrete objects, and describing location on a grid;
- recognize and use grade-appropriate vocabulary for these transformations; and
- have experience writing out explanations using symbols and numbers.

### Materials

blank paper
pencils
paper and scissors (to trace and cut out the shape)
mirrors (optional)

### Grouping Arrangement

Introduce the problem in a large group. Students will work individually on the task.

## Presenting the Problem

1. Explore and review the names of transformations. It would be beneficial to draw and post examples of each transformation in the classroom.

2. Using a grid similar to that in the investigation, create a simple image to model the requirements for this task. Have students create and cut out their own copy of the image.
3. Ask students one way to transform the image. Place one response in one of the quadrants of the grid. Ask students how to transform the new image. Place that response in the next quadrant of the grid. Challenge them to transform the new image so that the next transformation will provide the original image. Record the ideas. Brainstorm possible alternatives or corrections.
4. Display the question on the overhead. Discuss that they will be using the same steps as in Step 3 to transform the image, then must write directions for describing each transformation to a friend.
5. Encourage students to trace and cut out the original shape, and use this manipulative to help them.
6. Review the assessment criteria with students. Remind them that they must describe their transformations to a friend who cannot see what they have done. Suggest that they imagine that they are talking to a friend on the telephone or behind a divider. What will they say?

### Assessment Criteria

It is important to let students know what will be evaluated before they start their task. Tell them that you are interested in finding out:

- how well they transform shapes;
- what vocabulary they use to explain these transformations;
- whether they follow the shape sequentially;
- how clear and precise their instructions are; and
- how accurately they describe movements and locations.

### Prompts for Getting Started

Some students initially may have difficulty getting started in their thinking. Others may feel that they are done after drawing one or two transformations. Some prompts to help them continue in their investigation include:

- What shape is in the upper left quadrant?
- What are the different ways of transforming this shape? Show me. (Using the manipulative.)
- How might you first transform this shape?
- Where will you place the transformation?
- How can you describe this transformation and location?

## Assessing the Work

This assessment focusses on student knowledge and understanding of transformations and their ability to recreate the path of the shape and retell it in a clear and accurate manner. Students must understand the transformation process, and then apply this understanding by transforming a shape and clearly explaining how it was transformed. They must also be able to locate themselves on a grid and explain their location. Some students will move the shape clockwise around the grid; others will move counter-clockwise. Either direction is fine. The important thing is that they use a variety of transformations as they move around the grid. Ideally, they should explain how to transform the third figure they draw in order to produce the original drawing.

## Hints for Scoring a Response

Student responses are being assessed for the level of mathematical understanding they represent. As you assess each response, consider the following questions:

- Did the student need assistance to get started?
- Did the student need assistance to complete the task?
- Did the student use transformations in all sections of the grid?
- Are instructions presented in a sequential manner?
- Do they make sense?
- Are they accurate?
- Is the presentation clear?
- Does the student use grade-appropriate vocabulary and symbols?

## Scoring Rubric

See page 56.

## Consolidating Learning

1. A few days after the activity, provide the grid from the question to students. Use the same shape. Give clear step-by-step directions telling how to transform the shape and where to locate it. Move the shape around the grid using directions similar to those used by some of the higher-level responses from this investigation. At the end, show students the actual transformations and discuss their results. What was clear about your directions? What was unclear?
2. As a class, discuss the characteristics of good directions. Make a list of pointers to help students give better directions.
3. Ask students to take another look at their responses using the list produced in Step 2. Challenge them to use what they have learned to improve their directions.

## Follow-Up Activity

1. Have students draw a simple shape on a four-part grid. Ask them to transform the shape as they move it around the grid. Have them develop directions to help someone repeat their transformations and place the transformed shape in the correct location.
2. Place students in pairs. One member of the pair sits behind a divider and provides the instructions. The other member draws. At the end of the instructions, the partners compare the original to

what was drawn and discuss what could have made the directions better.

3. Have students change places so that the drawer becomes the explainer. Again, have students discuss how close the drawer came to reproducing the original and how to improve instructions.
4. Have students with extremely clear instructions provide them to the class while all students try to follow them. As a group, discuss the results.

INVESTIGATION 7

# Shape Game Rubric

Name________________________________ Date____________

| Expectations | Level 1 | Level 2 | Level 3 | Level 4 |
|---|---|---|---|---|
| **Problem Solving**<br><br>3m74, 3m57 | Demonstrates a very limited understanding of performing and describing transformations such as flips, slides, and turns. | Demonstrates a limited understanding of performing and describing transformations such as flips, slides, and turns. | Demonstrates a general understanding of performing and describing transformations such as flips, slides, and turns. | Demonstrates a thorough understanding of performing and describing transformations such as flips, slides, and turns. |
| **Understanding of Concepts**<br><br>3m57, 3m59 | Demonstrates a very limited understanding of transformational geometry using concrete materials and drawings. | Demonstrates a limited understanding of transformational geometry using concrete materials and drawings. | Demonstrates a good understanding of transformational geometry using concrete materials and drawings. | Demonstrates an extensive understanding of transformational geometry using concrete materials and drawings. |
| **Application of Procedures**<br><br>3m59, 3m75 | Uses a few explanations to describe location and movement on a grid, with many omissions and/or errors. | Uses some explanations to describe location and movement on a grid, with some omissions and/or errors. | Uses general explanations to describe location and movement on a grid, with few omissions and/or errors. | Uses accurate explanations to describe location and movement on a grid, with no or few very minor omissions and/or errors. |
| **Communication**<br><br>3m59, 3m60, 3m76 | Explains, with limited clarity how to get from one point to another on a grid. | Explains, with some clarity how to get from one point to another on a grid. | Explains clearly how to get from one point to another on a grid. | Explains clearly, precisely, and effectively, how to get from one point to another on a grid. |

• See CD-ROM for additional regional rubrics.

Comments:

**Level 4 Response**

Look at the creative and well organized way this student shows the transitions. Each move is clearly shown and labelled. Also notice the interesting idea of moving the shape diagonally in step 2. This response shows an accurate use of direction. Fractions are used appropriately and accurately.

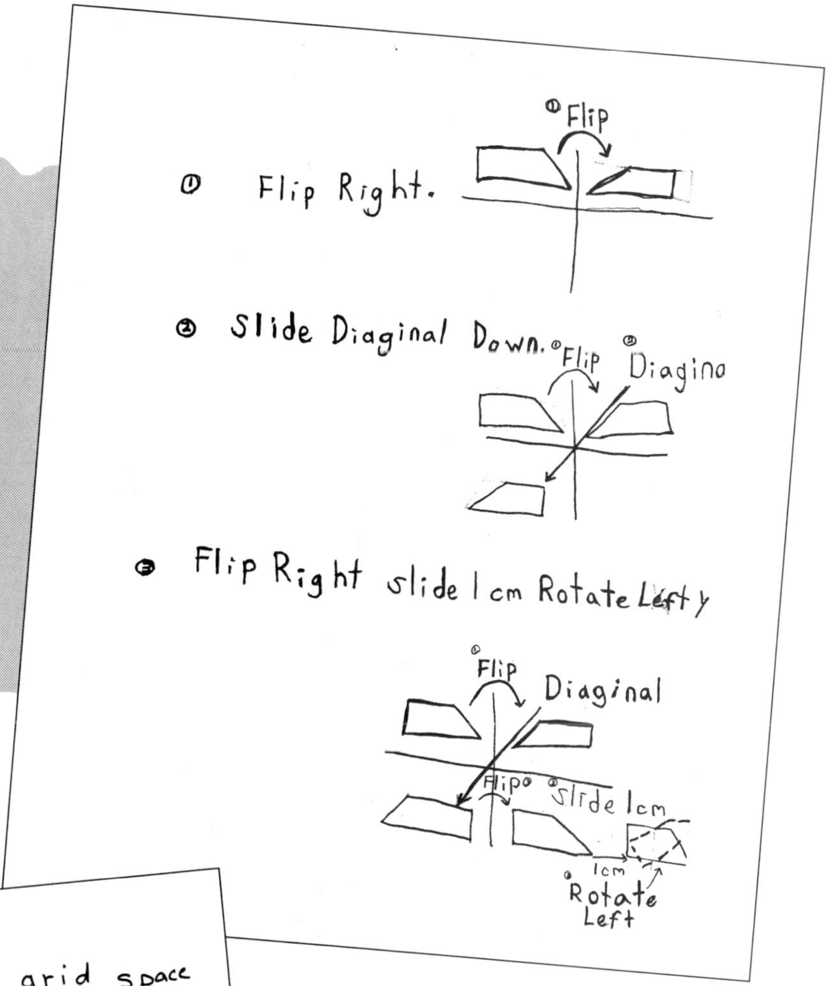


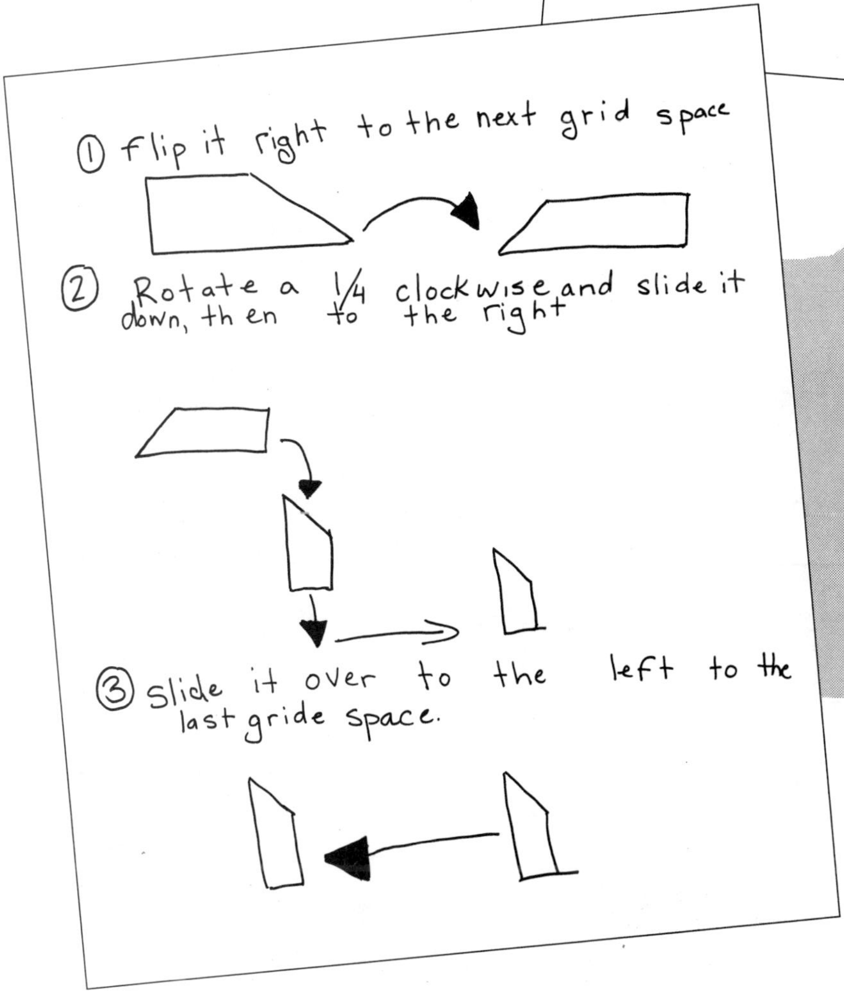


**Level 3 Response**

This is another interesting way of showing various transformations. The directions are correct and clear. Some math terms are used. The precision makes this a high level 3 response.

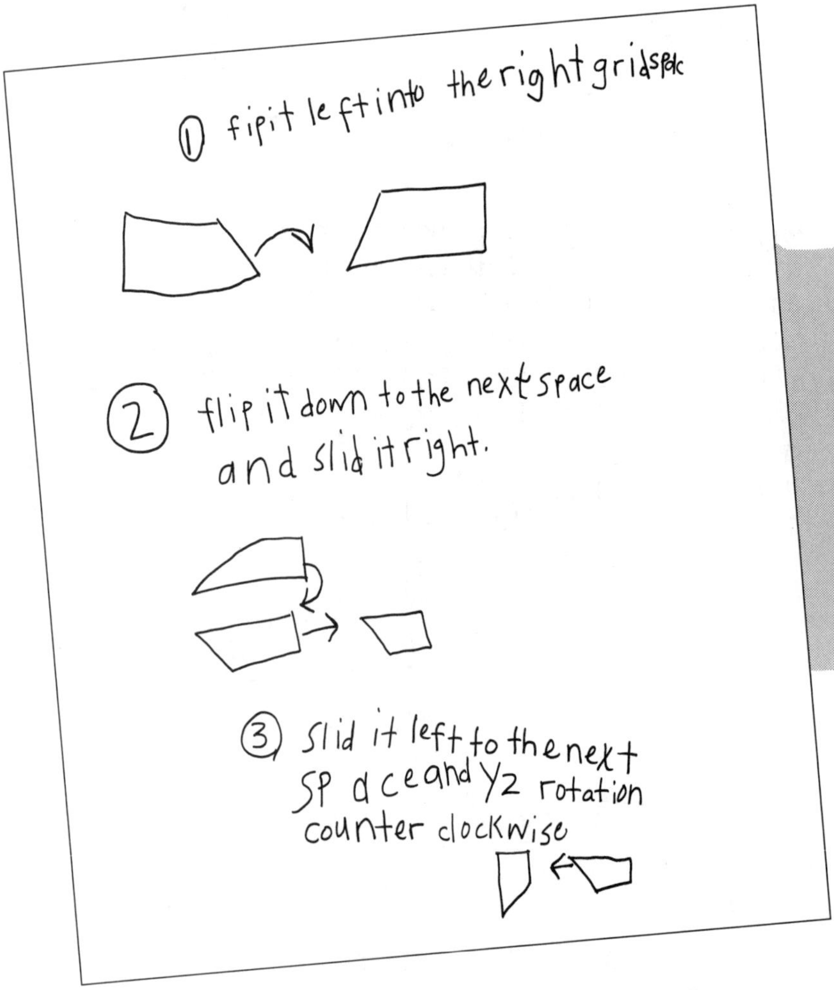


**Level 2 Response**

This student uses two terms correctly and uses directional instructions. The response illustrates some good thinking. The directional language is there, but not quite clear.

**Level 1 Response**

This student uses one simple transformation and uses it incorrectly. The shape is really being turned. The turn is not communicated.

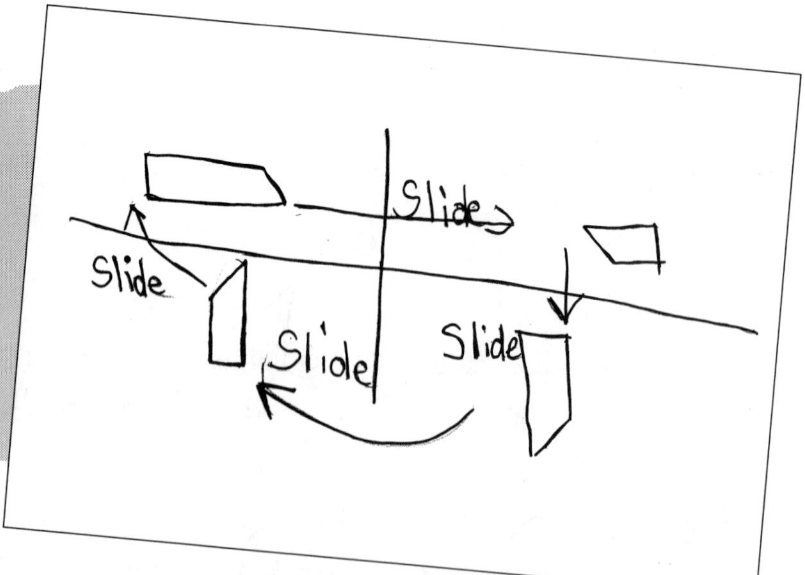

INVESTIGATION 8

# Pattern Game

**Focus: Patterning and Algebra**

This investigation challenges students to develop and draw three different number patterns. They are asked to use repeating, growing, and shrinking patterns, and to develop and justify a rule for each pattern. Students are asked to work with numbers less than 100, and can use a calculator to assist them with developing their patterns. The best way to assess the student's level of understanding is to examine the pattern rule(s) developed.

### Curriculum Expectations

- Identify, extend, and create linear and non-linear geometric patterns, number and measurement patterns, and patterns in their environment.
- Understand patterns in which operations are repeated, transformations are repeated, or multiple changes are made to attributes.
- Discuss the choice of a pattern rule.
- Use addition and subtraction facts to generate simple patterns in a hundreds chart.
- Identify relationships between addition, subtraction, multiplication, and division.

### Prior Knowledge/Skills

Students will need to have previous experience making simple number patterns, and will need to understand the idea of repeating (e.g., 1, 5, 7, 1, 5, 7, …), growing (e.g., 2, 4, 6, 8, …), and shrinking (e.g., 49, 42, 35, 28, …) number patterns.

### Materials

blank paper
pencils
crayons
calculator (optional)

### Grouping Arrangement

Introduce the problem in a large group. Students will work individually on the task.

## Presenting the Problem

1. Ask the students to think of a number pattern. Ask for some examples and display them on the chalkboard or chart paper. From the examples, choose one or more simple repeating, growing, and shrinking patterns. If the examples do not include each type, work with the class to develop several examples of the missing type. Discuss with the group what makes each type of pattern unique.

2. Show the question on an overhead and ask students to think about how they might answer the question. Discuss the ideas for a few minutes.
3. When most of the students are sure of what is expected, have them begin to plan, and then draw, their number patterns.
4. Have them assess their own drawings by asking questions such as:
    - Is this a pattern?
    - What kind of pattern is this?
    - How do I know that this is a repeating (or growing or shrinking) number pattern?
5. Once students seem to be finishing their drawings, ask them to think about the rule for their pattern and be prepared to communicate it.

### Assessment Criteria

It is important to let students know what will be evaluated before they start their task. Tell them that you are interested in finding out:

- that they can make patterns that repeat, grow, and shrink;
- that they can use different operations (e.g., +, –) in their patterns;
- that they can explain the pattern rule(s) for each of their drawings.

### Prompts for Getting Started

Some students initially may have difficulty getting started in their thinking. Others may feel that they are done after having presented only one type of pattern. Some prompts to help them continue in their investigation include:

- What is shown in the picture? What numbers are shown? What kind of pattern is this? How do you know? How can you use this pattern to help you make another one?
- Can you use numbers in another type of number pattern (i.e., repeating or shrinking)?
- This is an interesting pattern. (Pointing to a pattern.) Can you think of a way to make this pattern repeat (or grow or shrink)?
- Explain how you are making your pattern. What kind of pattern is this? How do you know?

## Assessing the Work

This assessment looks at the student's ability to devise number patterns that repeat, grow, and shrink. Some students may simply copy the illustrated pattern; others may use the same pattern but change the numbers. Some will focus on a repeated action or operation, such as adding or subtracting a number each time. A few students may not be able to articulate the pattern rule; others will explain or write it using correct terminology.

## Hints for Scoring a Response

Student responses are being assessed for the level of mathematical understanding they represent. As you assess each response, consider the following questions:

- Did the student need assistance to get started?
- Did the student need assistance to complete the task?
- How well does the student understand the idea of the three different types of patterns?
- How many different kinds of patterns did the student draw?
- How sophisticated is each pattern?
- What actions or operations are used? How complex are they?
- How clearly and accurately can the student explain the pattern rule?
- What mathematical terminology does the student use?
- How many prompts or directions does the student need to start and complete the task?

## Scoring Rubric

See page 62.

## Consolidating Learning

1. Display some of the higher-level or simple but interesting patterns that students develop and ask students to explain the pattern rule.
2. Display some higher-level responses. Discuss with a group, or the class, what makes these responses higher-level. For example, discuss how the patterns are more complex, may use addition and subtraction, and include a clear explanation of the pattern rule(s).
3. Ask students to take another look at their own work and plan one or two ways to change it to make it more like the higher-level examples.

## Follow-Up Activity

1. Ask the students to work in pairs. Have them develop several new patterns, show their patterns to their partner, and explain how the patterns work.
2. Extend the discussion to the whole class and discuss the examples that students have made. Challenge individuals to show the class how their patterns work.
3. Ask the students to work in pairs to make up three new number patterns, one of each type. Have them exchange patterns and classify each of the patterns they receive.
4. Challenge advanced students to develop repeating growing patterns or patterns that grow and then shrink.

# Investigation 8 Pattern Game Rubric

Name ______________________ Date __________

| Expectations | Level 1 | Level 2 | Level 3 | Level 4 |
|---|---|---|---|---|
| **Problem Solving**<br><br>3m78, 3m84 | Provides a few disconnected ideas by creating very simple number patterns with very little variety; needs considerable assistance to state pattern rules. | Provides some connected thoughts by creating simple number patterns with some variety; needs some assistance to state pattern rules. | Provides clear and independent thinking through effective number patterns with variety; correctly states pattern rules. | Provides a variety of complex patterns with some sophistication; states pattern rules correctly and precisely. |
| **Understanding of Concepts**<br><br>3m78, 3m81, 3m86, 3m88 | Demonstrates limited understanding by creating very simple patterns with very little variety. | Demonstrates some understanding by creating simple patterns with some variety; has minor errors. | Demonstrates considerable understanding by creating accurate patterns with variety. | Demonstrates an in-depth understanding by creating complex patterns with a lot of variety. |
| **Application of Procedures**<br><br>3m78, 3m81, 3m86, 3m88 | With considerable assistance, applies addition and subtraction in forming simple repeating, growing, and shrinking number patterns. | With some assistance, applies such functions as addition and subtraction in forming repeating, growing, and shrinking number patterns. | Independently applies such functions as addition and subtraction in forming repeating, growing, and shrinking number patterns. | Shows some sophistication in applying the most appropriate operation(s) to develop repeating, growing, and shrinking number patterns. |
| **Communication**<br><br>3m84 | Communicates a few ideas about patterns and pattern rules with limited accuracy and clarity. | Communicates some ideas about patterns and pattern rules with some accuracy and clarity. | Communicates patterns and pattern rules clearly and correctly. | Communicates ideas and states patterns and pattern rules with a high degree of accuracy, clarity, and precision. |

• See CD-ROM for additional regional rubrics.

Comments:

## Level 4 Response

This student shows considerable sophistication by combining the types of patterns. Instead of a simple growing pattern, she provides patterns that grow and then shrink. The repeating pattern also shows some sophistication as it does not simply repeat a series of numbers, but provides some elements of a growing pattern. The rules are stated simply, clearly, and concisely. There is a minor error in the second pattern. It should start and end with 10.

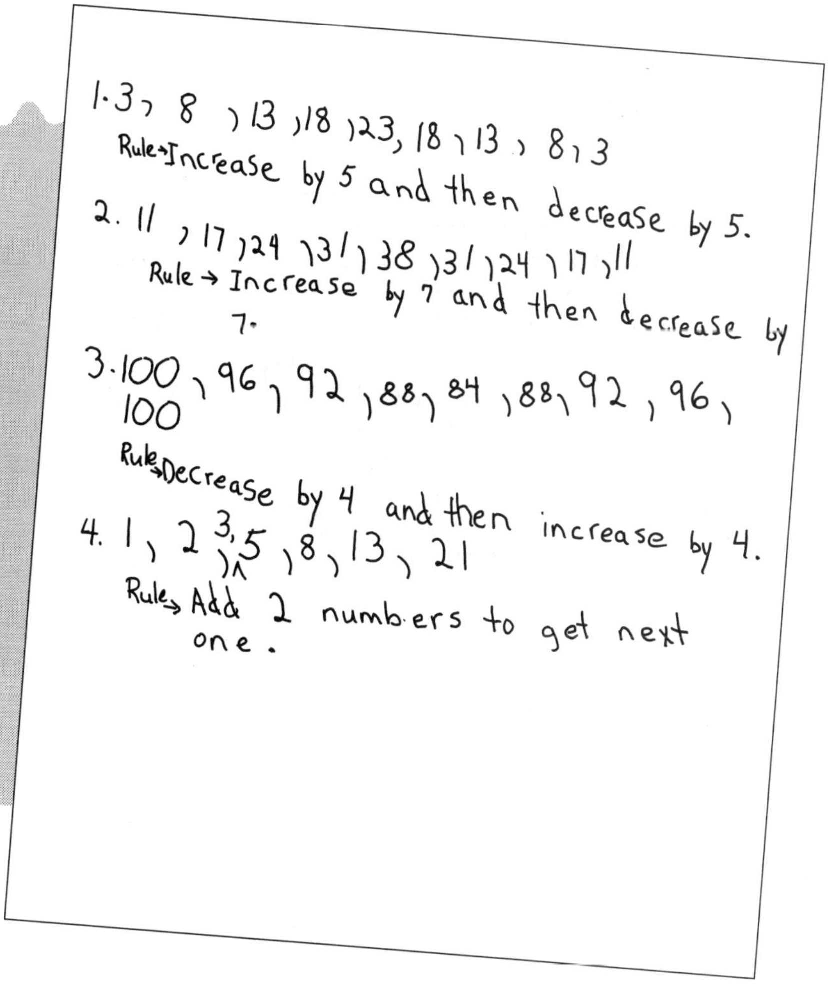
1. 3, 8, 13, 18, 23, 18, 13, 8, 3
Rule→Increase by 5 and then decrease by 5.
2. 11, 17, 24, 31, 38, 31, 24, 17, 11
Rule → Increase by 7 and then decrease by 7.
3. 100, 96, 92, 88, 84, 88, 92, 96, 100
Rule→Decrease by 4 and then increase by 4.
4. 1, 2, 3, 5, 8, 13, 21
Rule→ Add 2 numbers to get next one.

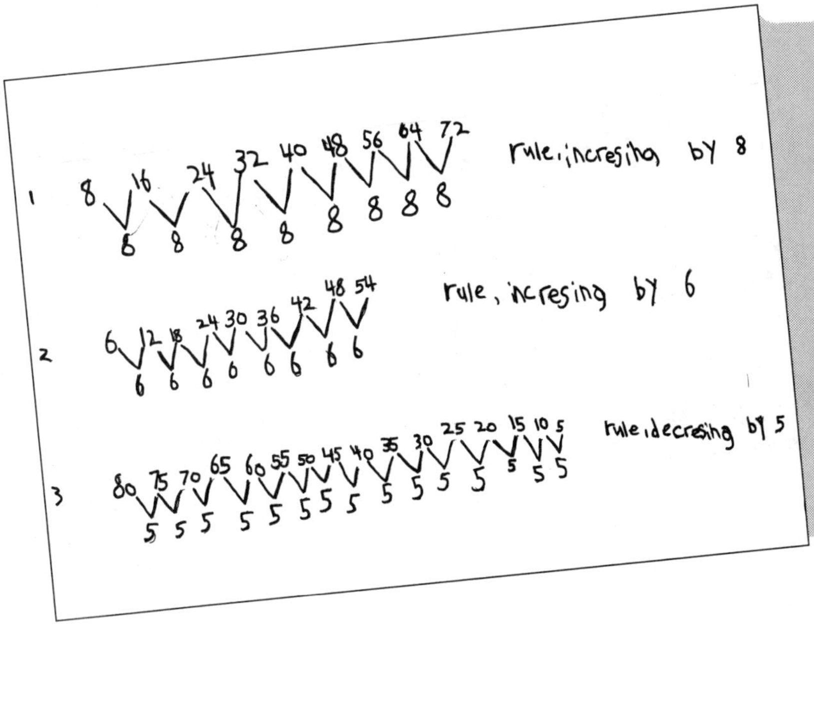


## Level 3 Response

This student provides clear and independent thinking as she correctly states the pattern rules for these increasing and decreasing patterns. The response displays considerable understanding as it shows accurate patterns with some variety. The patterns and pattern rules are communicated clearly and correctly.

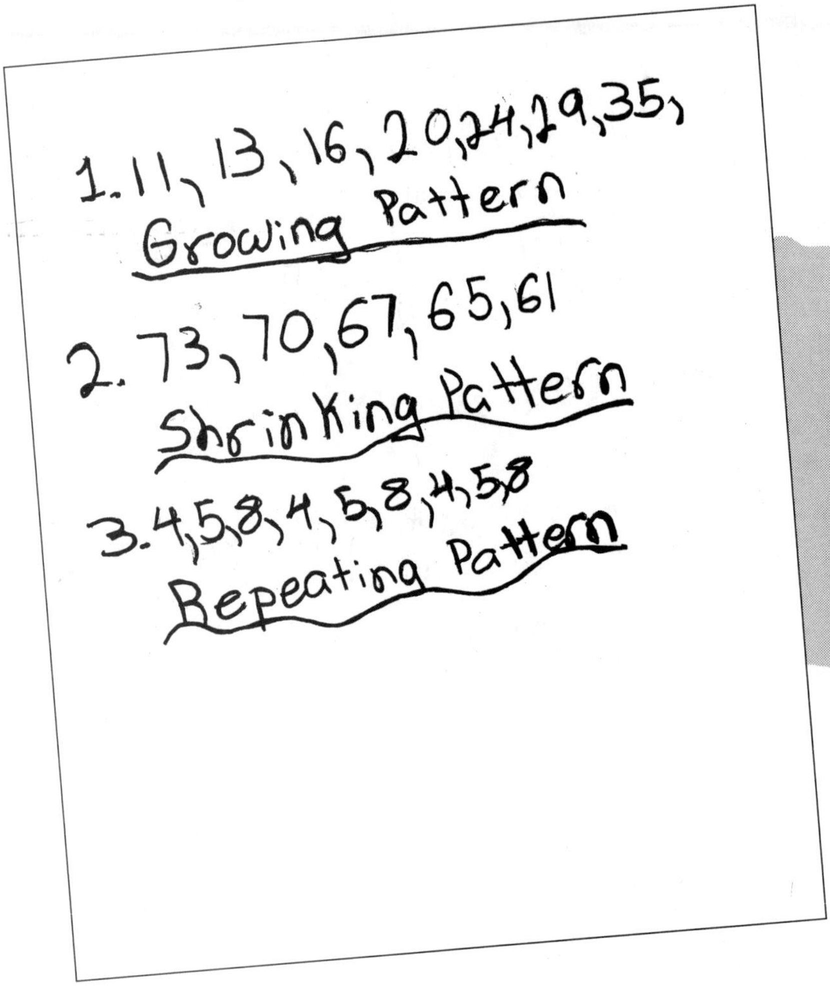


**Level 2 Response**

This student creates simple number patterns with minor errors. The student also correctly identifies the growing, shrinking, and repeating patterns. Note the use of both addition and subtraction in forming these number patterns.

**Level 1 Response**

This student creates simple patterns with some variety. The student demonstrates a limited understanding by creating very simple patterns and needs assistance in stating pattern rules. With considerable assistance, the student applies addition and subtraction in forming simple repeating, growing, and shrinking patterns. The accuracy of these patterns is limited.

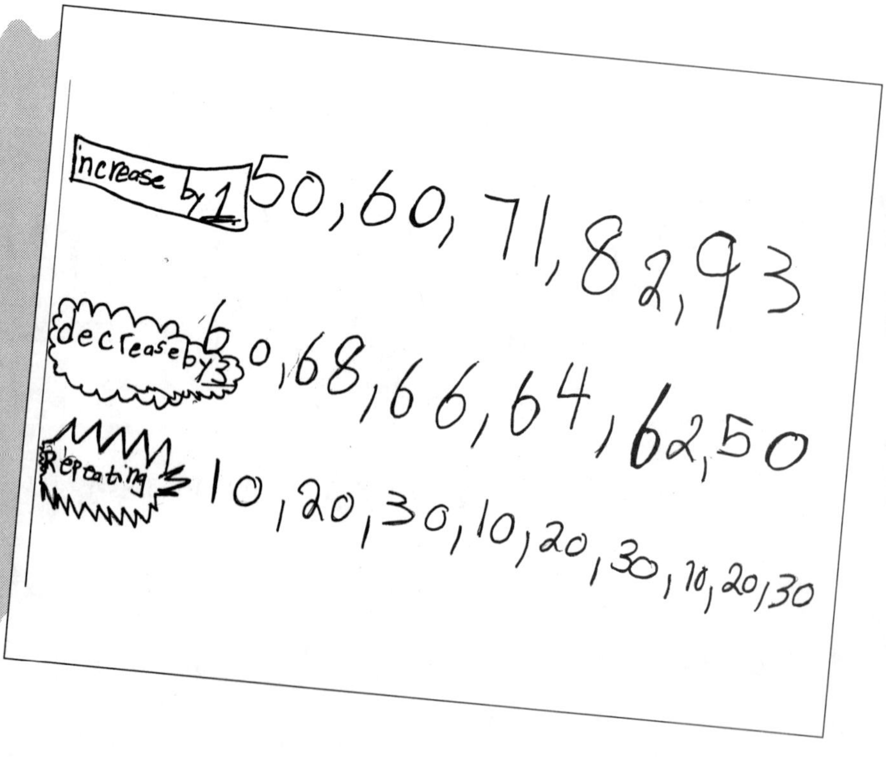

INVESTIGATION 9

# Milk Shake Flavours

**Focus: Data Management and Probability**

In this investigation, students are asked to determine what information is displayed on the pictograph, as well as what information is missing, and what may be missing. This is an open-ended question that encourages students to gather information from the visual, and then to speculate about what else *could* be there.

## Curriculum Expectations

- Sort, classify, and cross-classify objects and data.
- Interpret displays of data, present the information, and discuss it using mathematical language.
- Relate objects to number on a graph with many-to-one correspondence.
- Construct bar graphs and pictographs using scales with multiples of 2, 5, and 10.
- Interpret data from bar graphs, pictographs, and circle graphs.

## Prior Knowledge/Skills

Before doing this activity, students should have experience:

- creating and interpreting data for graphs;
- drawing, labelling, and analysing graphs; and
- using manipulatives as counters.

## Materials

blank paper
pencils
crayons
manipulatives such as buttons, bottle caps, and cubes

## Grouping Arrangement

Introduce the problem in a large group. Students will work individually on the task.

## Presenting the Problem

1. Make sure that students know what a pictograph is. To help them, review one they have recently done in class, covering up some of the information on the graph. Review the information displayed on the graph. Because very little numeric or textual information is provided on the graph here, it is necessary for the students to be familiar with the attributes of a graph.
2. Put the question on the overhead and read it aloud with the students. Discuss the visual.

3. Work with the class to start a list of information shown on the graph.
4. Point out that students are asked to show all of the information that the graph provides, to figure out what is missing, and then to complete the graph. Explain that there may be more than one way to complete the graph. For example, perhaps some of the data is missing.
5. Review the assessment criteria with the students. Make sure they understand what you are looking for in the answer.

### Assessment Criteria

It is important to let the students know what will be evaluated in this assessment. Tell them you are interested in finding out:

- how much information they are able to get from the graph;
- whether they are able to use manipulatives to interpret the data;
- whether they are able to determine what information is missing from the data;
- how well they complete the graph; and
- if they can provide more than one solution.

### Prompts for Getting Started

Some students initially may have difficulty getting started in their thinking. Others may feel that they are done after copying the list of data you prepared with the class or after explaining what is missing from the graph. Some prompts to help them continue in their investigation include:

- Who made this graph?
- What do you think the graph is supposed to show?
- How could you make the message clearer?
- Might the maker have forgotten to display some data? What might this include? How might you show it?
- What other data might be on this graph?
- Are there special terms you might use when discussing this graph?
- Is there another way you could complete this graph?

## Assessing the Work

This question assesses how well students can analyse data from a partial graph, identify what is missing, and then complete the graph. Some students will provide only one way to complete the graph; others will suggest various ways the graph could be completed by labelling it in different ways or adding data. Also, the graph could be a vertical or horizontal bar graph. Students may orient the bars either way as they fix the graph. Encourage students to use manipulatives and observe their strategy(ies) for doing so.

## Hints for Scoring a Response

Student responses are being assessed for the level of mathematical understanding they demonstrate. As you assess each response, consider the following questions:

- Did the student need assistance to get started?
- Did the student need assistance to complete the task?
- How much information does the student gather?
- How complex is this information?
- How well does the student use manipulatives?
- How many different kinds of information does the student list?
- How much of the missing information is the student able to determine?
- How well does the student extrapolate what *might* be on the graph from what is currently on the graph?
- How many ways can the student complete the graph?

## Scoring Rubric

See rubric on page 68.

## Consolidating Learning

1. Gather the students together to share their work and the thinking they used in this investigation.
2. Display a higher-level response and review the criteria that made it a higher-level answer. Ask students to use this discussion and take a look at their own response. Can they add information to make it a higher-level one?
3. Match up students who have a higher-level response, one on one, with those who have a lower-level response. Use this peer coaching to assist students with the lower-level response in upgrading that response.

## Follow-Up Activity

1. Have individual students collect their own data by conducting a survey. For example: What is your favourite pet?
2. Have students tally their responses and give their tally sheets to a partner. The partner then creates a graph that reflects all of the data collected on the tally sheet.
3. Have a third student review the tally sheet and graph, and assess whether any attributes or information are missing from the graph. The student should complete or correct the graph.
4. Alternatively, have students survey individuals about which of two animals they prefer, or whether they have no preference. Have students use a Venn diagram to show the results.

# Investigation 9 Milk Shake Flavours Rubric

Name ______________________________ Date ____________

| Expectations | Level 1 | Level 2 | Level 3 | Level 4 |
|---|---|---|---|---|
| **Problem Solving**<br><br>3m90, 3m92 | Demonstrates a very limited understanding. With a lot of assistance, interprets what information is displayed and what missing. | Demonstrates some understanding. With some assistance, interprets what information is displayed and what is missing. | Demonstrates a general understanding of what information is displayed and what missing. | Demonstrates a clear and thorough understanding of what information is displayed and what missing. |
| **Understanding of Concepts**<br><br>3m99, 3m102 | With a lot of assistance, interprets some of the data and identifies and discusses some of the basic information that is missing. | With limited assistance, interprets some of the data and identifies and discusses some of the numeric and textual information that is missing. | Interprets most of the data; identifies most of the missing numeric and textual information. | Provides a clear and thorough interpretation of the data; identifies what numeric and textual information is missing. |
| **Application of Procedures**<br><br>3m101, 3m102 | With assistance, identifies some of the basic parts of the graph and partially fixes the graph, with some major errors. | With limited assistance, identifies many basic parts of the graph; uses this to identify some of the missing information, with minor errors. | Independently identifies the majority of the parts of a graph; uses this information to identify most or all of the missing information. | Clearly identifies all parts of the graph; uses this to thoroughly identify all of the missing information; provides more than one appropriate solution. |
| **Communication**<br><br>3m92 | Interprets displays of information on the graph and expresses understanding of the data in a limited manner. | Interprets the data displayed on the graph and expresses understanding of the missing data in a simple manner. | Interprets the data displayed and expresses understanding of the majority of missing information with some accuracy and using appropriate terminology. | Interprets the data and expresses a thorough understanding of the information in a variety of ways and using appropriate terminology. |

• See CD-ROM for additional regional rubrics.

Comments:

**Level 4 Response**

This response demonstrates a clear and thorough understanding of what information is displayed and what is missing. The student provides more than one solution, showing a good understanding of how graphs work. Note how the data is shown both horizontally and vertically. This student uses appropriate terminology and clearly expresses what needs to be fixed.

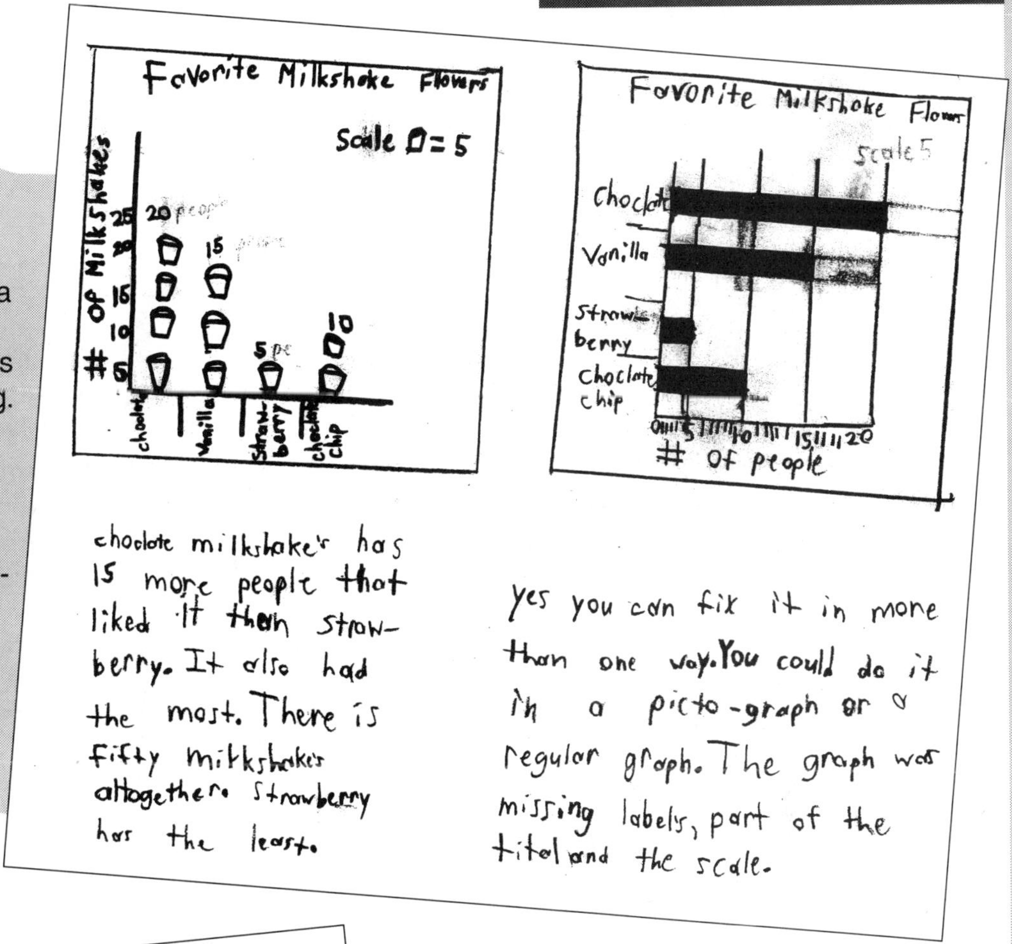


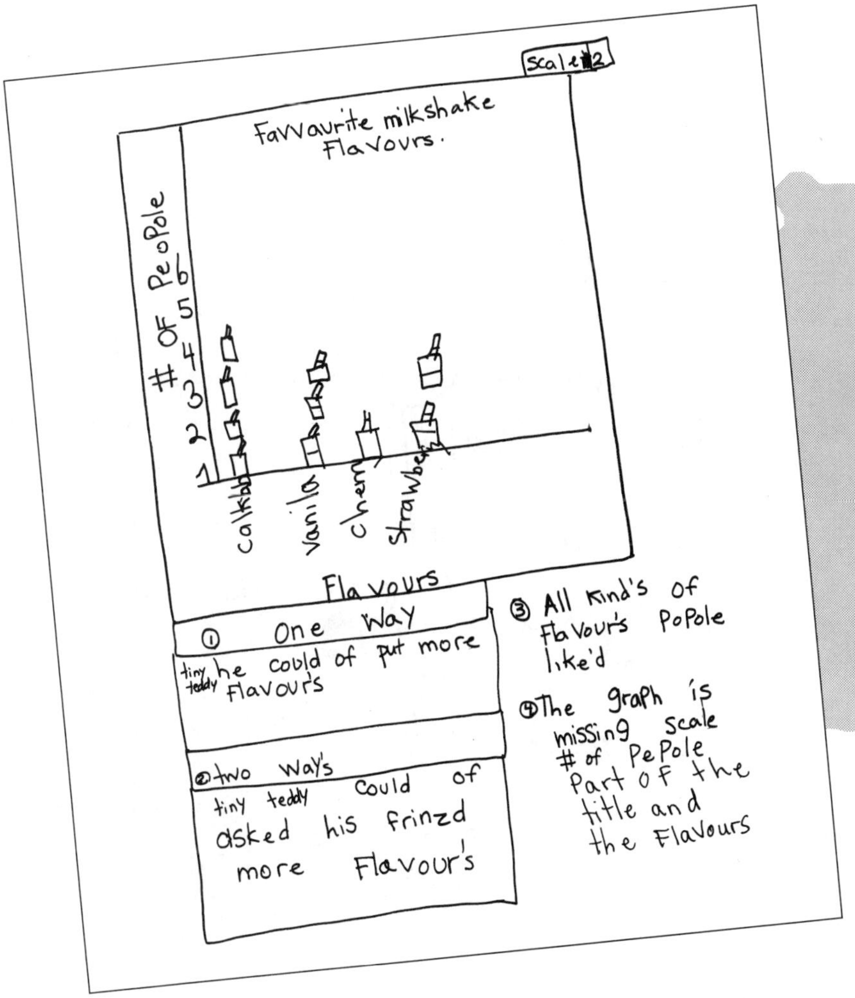


**Level 3 Response**

This student demonstrates a general understanding of what is displayed and what missing. Notice how the response identifies most of the missing numeric and textual information, and provides most of the parts of a graph. The student uses appropriate terminology. The response does not interpret data numerically.

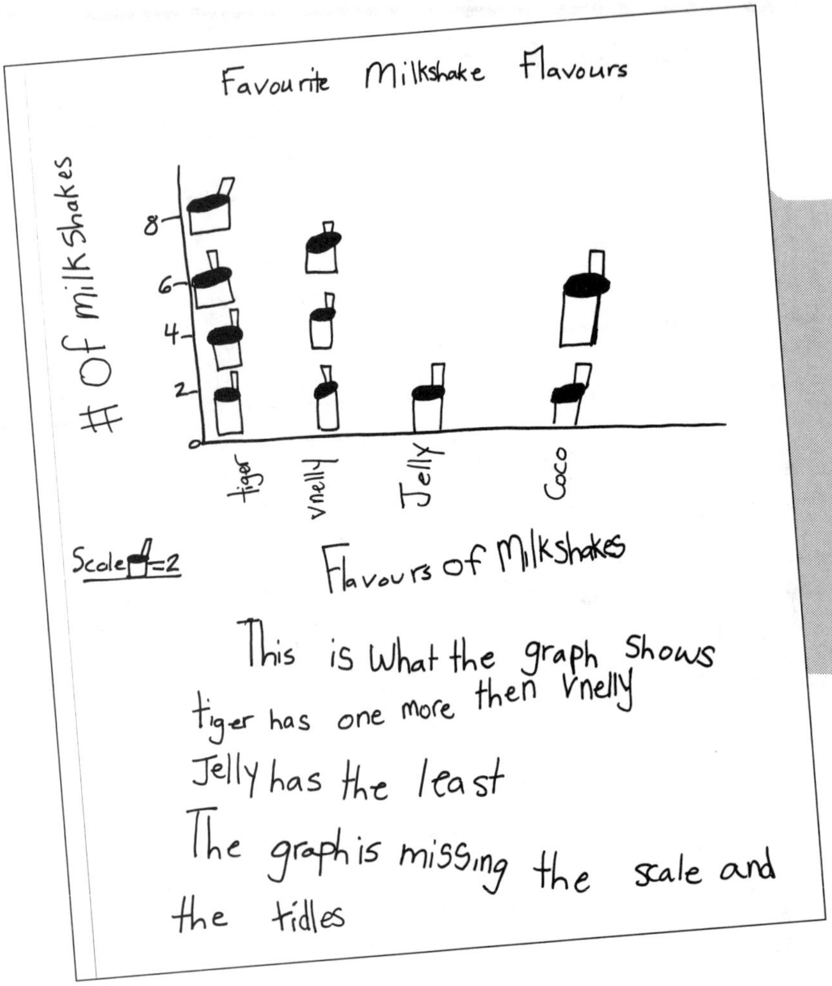


**Level 2 Response**

This student demonstrates some understanding of the information on the graph. The response interprets some of the numeric and textual information. The student also communicates that some of the information is missing; i.e., the scale and title.

**Level 1 Response**

This student demonstrates a very limited understanding, with no interpretation of data. The communication is limited to labelling the graph.

Investigation 10

# Who Will Win?

## Focus: Data Management and Probability

In this investigation, students are asked to understand a simple two-person game, to assess which player has a better chance of winning, and to explain that choice. The game is clearly weighted so that one player has a better chance of winning, but there is a distractor in the four green crayons that really have nothing to do with the outcome of the game. Students are asked to suggest changes that will make the game more fair. When doing this, students need to consider the game in terms of "likely to win," "possibly win," and "more likely to win." Player 1 has four out of ten chances of getting a red crayon and is likely to win. Player 2 has two out of ten chances of getting a blue crayon and is less likely to win. Some students may point out that Player 1 is twice as likely to win.

### Curriculum Expectations

- Demonstrate an understanding of probability and the ability to apply probability in familiar day-to-day situations.
- Conduct simple probability experiments and predict the results.
- Apply the concept of likelihood of events in solving simple problems.
- Use mathematical language to describe probability.

### Prior Knowledge/Skills

Students should have some experience:

- playing and thinking about a variety of games of chance;
- using appropriate language to describe games and events; and
- using probability terms such as "likely," "possibly," and "more likely."

Prior to this activity, they should have used pictures, words, and numbers to communicate their understanding in other situations.

### Materials

blank paper
pencils
*Items for each pair*
bag ( preferably cloth bag with a draw string)
4 red crayons
4 green crayons
2 blue crayons

### Grouping Arrangement

Introduce the problem in a large group. Place students in pairs to experience the game. Students will work individually to complete the task.

## Presenting the Problem

1. Place the question on the overhead with the visual covered up. Read the game rules to students. Demonstrate how to play a game similar to the one illustrated but using a different combination of numbers of crayons. Discuss this game and whether both players have an equal chance of winning.
2. Uncover the visual. Reread the game rules to students and discuss how the game is played.
3. Have the students play the game in pairs, each taking a turn to be Player 1 and Player 2.
4. Ask the students to consider who they would prefer to be in the game: Player 1 or Player 2. Ask them to state and write their choice of players to be and explain why they made it.
5. Ask the students to consider whether both players have an equal chance of winning the game here. If they do not, challenge them to change the game to give both players an equal chance.

### Assessment Criteria

It is important to let students know what they will be evaluated on before they start their task. Tell them that you are interested in finding out:

- which player they would like to be in the game — and why;
- their opinion of whether both players have an equal chance — and why they think this way; and
- if they think that both players do not have an equal chance, their ideas for changing the game to give both players a chance to win.

### Prompts for Getting Started

Some students initially may have difficulty getting started in their thinking. Others may feel that they are done after having presented which player they would like to be, and possibly why. Some prompts to help them continue in their investigation include:

- What colours are the crayons? How many are there of each colour?
- Try putting the same combination of colours of crayons in a bag to see which ones are pulled out. Which colour was pulled out most often?
- Which player do you think has the best chance of getting the needed colour? Is the game fair? Why or why not?
- Which player would you like to be? Why?
- How would you change the game to make it fair?
- Is there any other way you could change the game to give each player a chance of winning?

## Assessing the Work

When assessing student responses, look for evidence of understanding that probability is not random but is based on reason, and ways of changing the game to equalize chances of winning.

### Hints for Scoring a Response

Student responses are being assessed for the level of mathematical understanding they represent. As you assess each response, consider the following questions:

- Did the student need assistance to get started?
- Did the student need assistance to complete the task?
- Did the student give one or more reasons for player selection? How clear and appropriate are the justifications?
- Was the student able to change the game to make it fair?
- Did the student show different ways to change the game?
- Did the student clearly explain the thinking involved?

## Scoring Rubric

See page 74.

## Consolidating Learning

1. Share some of the higher-level responses with the class and have students explain what makes these levels 3 and 4.
2. Have students look back at their own work. Have them try the changes they made to the game to see if they worked to make the game fair.
3. Have students assess what qualities their work shares with the level 3 or 4 samples. What is different?
4. Suggest that students make any changes they think would improve their original work.

## Follow-Up Activity

1. In pairs, have students carry out a similar task drawing different objects from a box. Have them discuss which player they want to be and why.
2. Have them change the game to make it fair, and then check whether their plan works. To do this, they could draw items 10 times each and tally the score.
3. Have pairs share with the class the work they have completed.

# Who Will Win? Rubric

INVESTIGATION 10

Name ________________________ Date ____________

| Expectations | Level 1 | Level 2 | Level 3 | Level 4 |
|---|---|---|---|---|
| **Problem Solving**<br><br>3m93 | Demonstrates limited understanding by not providing a clear reason. | Demonstrates some understanding by selecting a player based on a somewhat clear reason. | Demonstrates a general understanding by selecting Player 1 based on a valid reason. | Demonstrates a thorough understanding by selecting Player 1 based on a clearly valid reason. |
| **Understanding of Concepts**<br><br>3m93 | Demonstrates a limited understanding of probability by not elaborating about why more red than blue crayons means that one player has a better chance. | Demonstrates some understanding of probability by providing a somewhat clear explanation and providing a simple or somewhat clear way to change the game. | Demonstrates general understanding by clearly explaining that more red than blue crayons increases the chances of winning and providing a clear way of changing the game. | Demonstrates a thorough understanding by clearly and concisely explaining what is wrong with the original game, and providing more than one clear way to change the game to make it fair. |
| **Application of Procedures**<br><br>3m103, 3m104 | With assistance, applies probability ideas (likely, unlikely, probably) to the game. | With limited assistance, applies probability ideas (likely, unlikely, probably) to the game. | Independently, applies probability ideas (likely, unlikely, probably). | Applies probability ideas to explain the change to the game and how it will equalize the chances of winning. |
| **Communication**<br><br>3m106 | Gives little or no explanation of choice of player or how to make the game more fair. | Gives some explanation of choice of player or how to make the game more fair. | Gives a clear explanation of choice of player and how to make the game more fair. | Gives a clear and precise explanation of the reason for the choice of player and changes to make the game more fair. |

• See CD-ROM for additional regional rubrics.

Comments:

**Level 4 Response**

This student demonstrates good use of probability language in clearly explaining why the game is unfair and providing ways of changing the game to make it fair. The response provides more than one clear way to change the game. Notice the creative revision that makes the game fair for three players!

> I would ratherbe playernumber one because you have a better chance of winning because there is four reds and only 2 blue so your more likley to pick out a red than a blue. This game isn't fair because if you are player two than you wouldn't really pick out blue offin where as player one usuwaly picks out red. because there is 2 blues and 4 reds and plus you addin 4 green so it isn't very fair for player two. The three things I would change in this game. First I would add two blue crayons. That would make it fair for player 2. Second I would just use one of each colour. So three people can play together, I would put two more blue in so there will be 4 reds, 4 greens and 4 blue so it's equle between everybody.

> I would like to be player one because player one has a better chance. You can change the game by putting in more blue blocks. You can put in less red. The game is not fair because player one has more red blocks then player twos blue blocks. Another change is player one gets green and player two is red

**Level 3 Response**

This response displays a high level of thinking. The reasons are phrased clearly. The student provides a good idea for changing the game to make it fair for both players. There is another interesting idea in which players switch places to give the losing player a chance to win. This suggestion does not equalize the chances of both players winning the game. The response is clear.

I want to be player 1 becose player 2 has more crayons. I think its unfair becose player 1 has more crayons. I want player 2 has 2 more crayons,

**Level 2 Response**

This student provides a correct and basic answer. The response uses little probability vocabulary. The student provides a simple way to change the game. The idea is not clear.

**Level 1 Response**

This student is thinking about probability. Her response has been side-tracked by other issues. Notice the interesting method she suggests for changing the game. This way might work to make the game fair, but is not explained.

I would like to be player one becuase ... it would let me have mose ponts if the other player gets it rong.
It is not fair becuase player one or two could look into the bag and chete. to grab the crayon they need.
My changes would be to make each crayon stand for a difrent pont. Make the players close ther eyes so they dont see. The player that wins can go on to a nathe playre that won. That player that had beten all of they other playres would go on and would fase friends from diffrent grads.

Name ______________________ Date ________________

INVESTIGATION 1

## The Jelly Bean Problem

How would you find out how many jelly beans there are?

Show as many different ways as you can. You may use pictures, words, and numbers.

1 2 3 4

Self Assessment

Nom ______________________________ Date ____________________

RECHERCHE 1

## Le probléme des bonbons à la gelée

Comment peux-tu trouver le nombre de bonbons à la gelée dans ces pots?

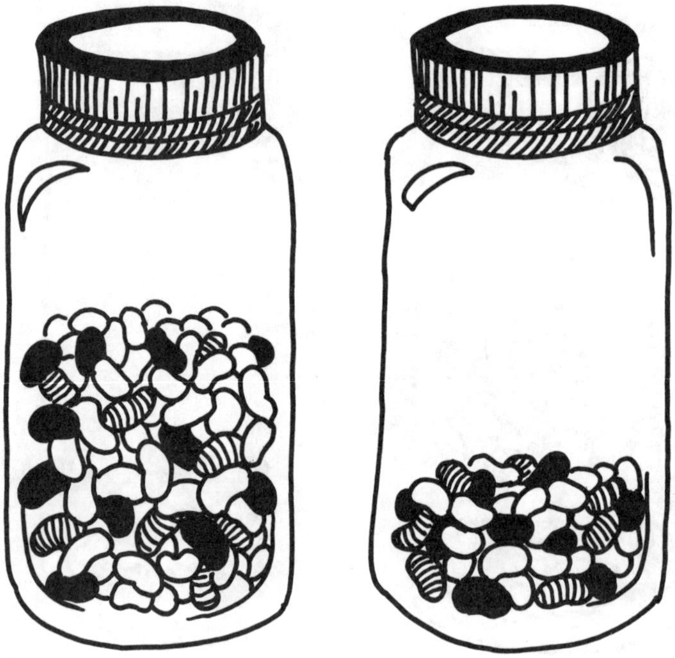

Montre autant de façons différentes que tu peux. Tu peux te servir d'images, de mots, et de nombres.

1 2 3 4

Autoévaluation

Name ______________________________ Date ____________________

**INVESTIGATION 2**

## Packing Cookies

You have 24 cookies to sell at your school's bake sale. Show all the ways to package these cookies.

You may use pictures, words, and numbers.

Nom ______________________________ Date ____________________

RECHERCHE 2

## L'emballage de biscuits

Tu as 24 biscuits à vendre à la vente de ton école. Montre toutes les façons possibles d'emballer ces biscuits.

Tu peux te servir d'images, de mots, et de nombres.

1 2 3 4

Autoévaluation

Name ______________________ Date ________________

INVESTIGATION 3

## Share With Friends

How will you share the chocolate bars fairly?

Show and write all the ways you can think of. You may use pictures, words, and numbers.

| 1 | 2 | 3 | 4 |
|---|---|---|---|

Self Assessment

Nom ______________________ Date ________________

## Partage avec des camarades

Comment peux-tu partager les barres de chocolat de façon équitable?

Montre et écris toutes les façons que tu peux imaginer. Tu peux te servir d'images, de mots, et de nombres.

Autoévaluation

Name ____________________ Date ____________________

INVESTIGATION 4

## Measure a Friend

How would you measure a snowman?

Show and write all the ways you can think of to measure it. You may use pictures, words, and numbers.

Nom ______________________________ Date ____________________

RECHERCHE 4

## La mesure

Comment peux-tu mesurer un bonhomme de neige?

Montre et écris toutes les façons de le mesurer que tu peux imaginer. Tu peux te servir d'images, de mots, et de nombres.

1 2 3 4

Autoévaluation

Name ______________________ Date ____________________

INVESTIGATION 5

## Money Equations

You have $5. How will you spend it?

Use the catalogue. Show different ways to spend your money. List the things you bought. Do you get any change?

1 2 3 4

Self Assessment

Nom ______________________________ Date ____________________

RECHERCHE 5

## Des équations d'argent

Tu as 5 $. Comment les dépenses-tu?

À partir du catalogue, montre différentes façons de dépenser ton argent. Dresse une liste des articles que tu achètes. Est-ce qu'on te rend de la monnaie?

1 | 2 | 3 | 4

Autoévaluation

Name ______________________________ Date ____________________

## Sort Shapes

How would you sort these shapes?

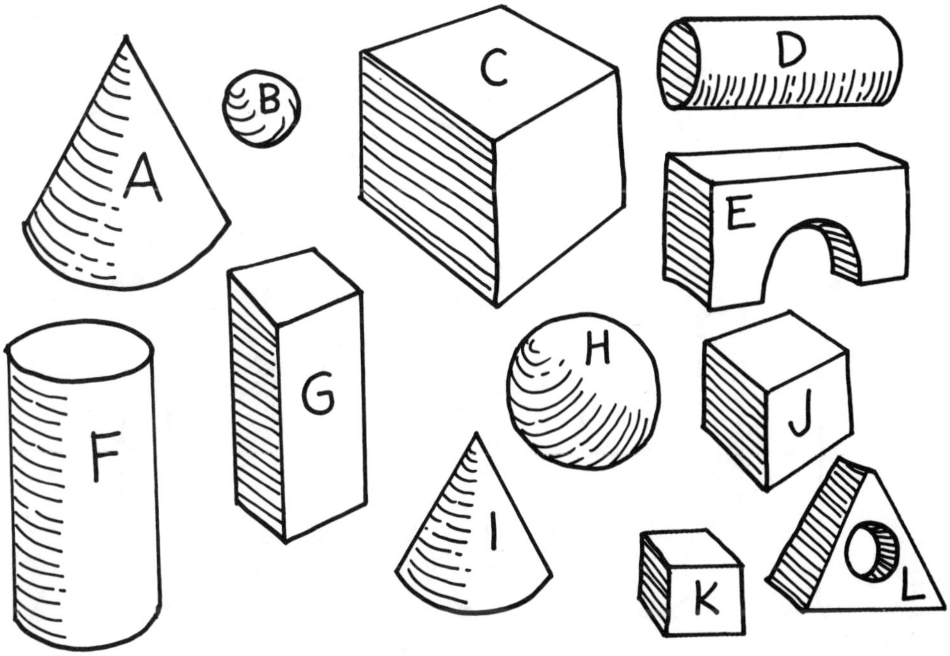


Show lots of different ways to sort them. Which sorting rules did you use?

Nom ______________________ Date ______________

RECHERCHE 6

## Classe des solides

Comment peux-tu classer ces solides?

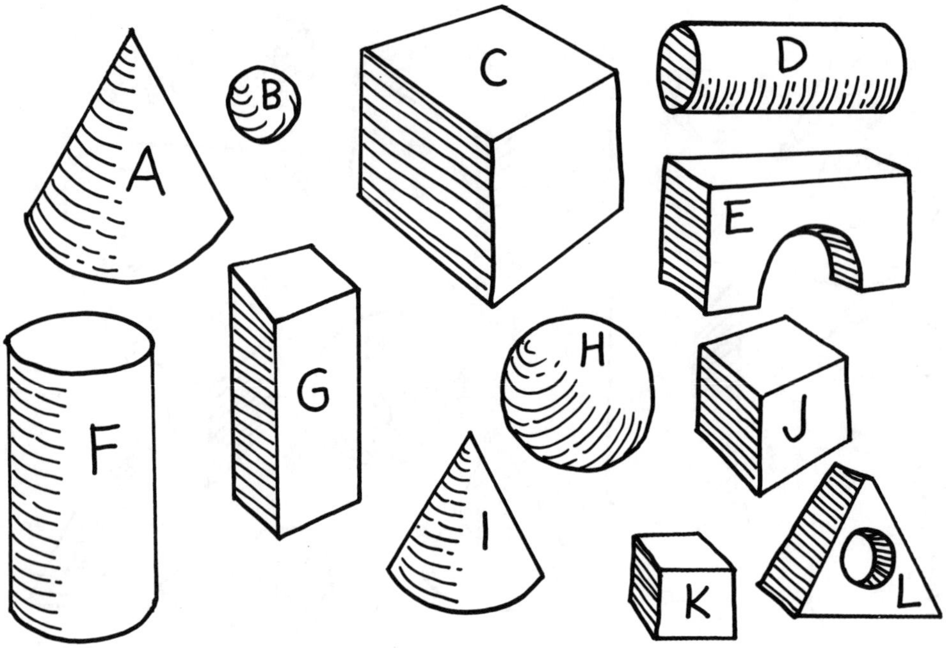


Montre beaucoup de façons différentes de les classer. Quelles règles de classification utilises-tu?

1 2 3 4

Autoévaluation

Name ______________________________ Date ____________________

INVESTIGATION 7

## Shape Game

Imagine you are talking to a friend who cannot see you. How would you tell your friend to move from one section of the grid to the next?

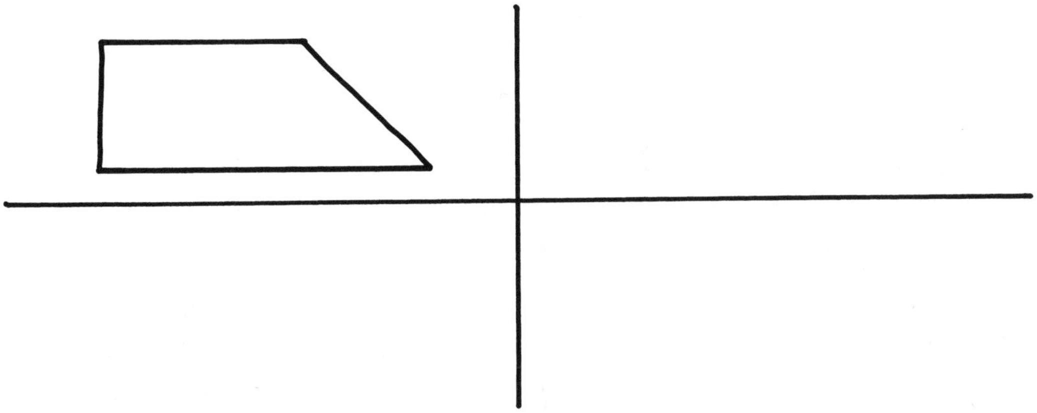

Use mathematical language. Tell your friend how to transform this image. How would it change in each section? You may use pictures, words, and symbols.

Nom ______________________________ Date ____________________

## Recherche 7 — Le jeu des figures

Imagine que tu parles à une personne qui ne peut pas te voir. Comment peux-tu lui expliquer de se déplacer d'une partie de la grille à l'autre?

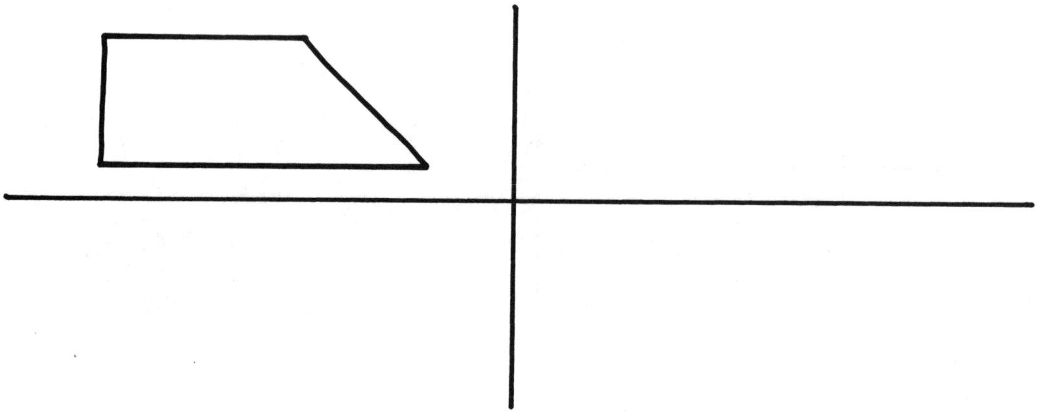

Utilise le langage mathématique. Dis à la personne comment transformer cette figure. Comment l'image de la figure apparaîtra-t-elle dans chaque partie de la grille? Tu peux te servir d'images, de mots, et de symboles.

Autoévaluation

Name ______________________ Date ______________

INVESTIGATION 8

## Pattern Game

Make up three different kinds of patterns.

Use repeating, growing, and shrinking patterns. Think about combining patterns. Write the rule for each pattern.




Self Assessment

Nom ______________________________ Date ____________________

RECHERCHE 8

## Le jeu des suites

Forme trois sortes de suites différentes.

Conçois des suites répétitives, croissantes, et décroissantes. Pense à combiner les suites. Écris la régularité pour chaque suite.

1 2 3 4

Autoévaluation

Name ______________________ Date ______________________

INVESTIGATION 9

## Milk Shake Flavours

What does this graph show? What is missing?

Tiny Teddy graphed his friends' favourite milk shake flavours. Then he spilled his milk shake all over it. Can you help him fix his graph? Can you fix it in more than one way?

Nom ______________________ Date ______________

RECHERCHE 9

## Les parfums de lait fouetté

Qu'est-ce que ce diagramme montre?
Qu'est-ce qui manque?

Petit Ours a fait un diagramme pour montrer les parfums de lait fouetté préférés de ses camarades. Il est triste, car il a renversé son lait fouetté dessus. Peux-tu l'aider à réparer son diagramme? Peux-tu le faire de plus d'une façon?

1 2 3 4
Autoévaluation

Name ______________________ Date ________________

INVESTIGATION 10

## Who Will Win?

Which player would you like to be? Why? How can you change the game to give the other player a better chance of winning?

### Game Rules

- Take turns picking a crayon from the bag.
- Player 1 wins 1 point if the crayon says red.
- Player 2 wins 1 point if the crayon says blue.
- No points for a green crayon.

1 2 3 4

Self Assessment

Nom ______________________ Date ______________

RECHERCHE 10

## Qui va gagner?

Aimerais-tu être à la place de A ou de B? Pourquoi? Comment peux-tu changer le jeu pour donner à l'autre personne de meilleures chances de gagner?

**Règles du jeu**

- À tour de rôle, A et B tirent un crayon du sac.
- A obtient 1 point si le crayon porte le mot rouge.
- B obtient 1 point si le crayon porte le mot bleu.
- Il n'y a pas de point si le crayon porte le mot vert.

1 2 3 4

Autoévaluation

## Problem Solving Model

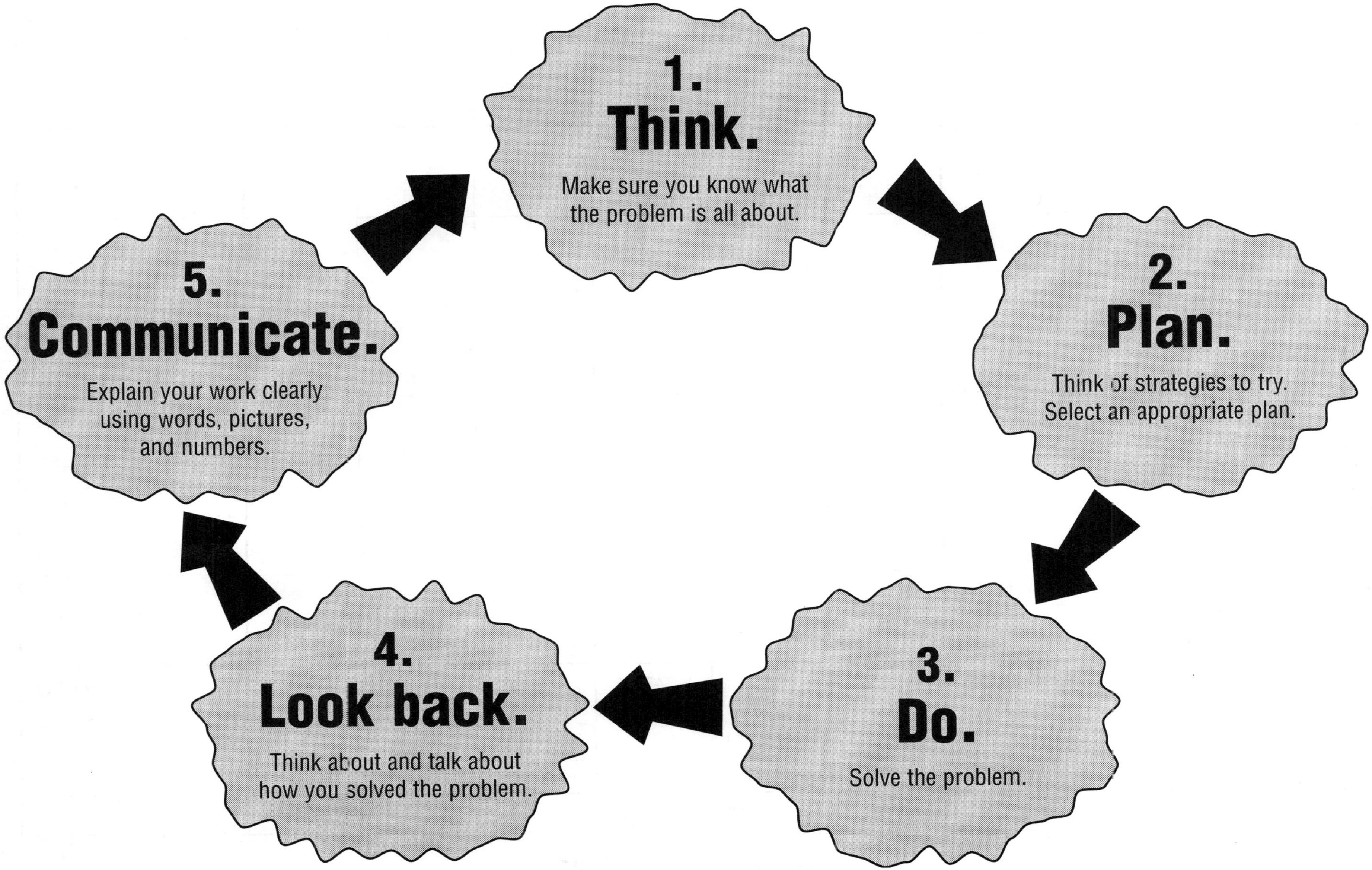

# Observation Checklist

| | Investigation #____ | | | Investigation #____ | | | |
|---|---|---|---|---|---|---|---|
| Name | Amount of Assistance<br>1 = a lot<br>2 = some<br>3 & 4 = independently | Use of concrete materials<br>I = inappropriate<br>A = appropriate | Collaboration<br>I = inappropriate<br>A = appropriate | Amount of Assistance<br>1 = a lot<br>2 = some<br>3 & 4 = independently | Use of concrete materials<br>I = inappropriate<br>A = appropriate | Collaboration<br>I = inappropriate<br>A = appropriate | Comments |
| | | | | | | | |
| | | | | | | | |
| | | | | | | | |
| | | | | | | | |
| | | | | | | | |
| | | | | | | | |
| | | | | | | | |
| | | | | | | | |

# Correlation to Canadian Curricula Grade 3

| Puddle Question | Ontario Expectations | Atlantic Provinces Education Foundation (APEF) Outcomes | Western Canadian Protocol (WCP) Specific Outcomes | British Columbia Integrated Resource Package (IRP) Outcomes |
|---|---|---|---|---|
| **1. The Jelly Bean Problem** | 3m1 represent whole numbers using concrete materials, drawings, numerals, and number words<br>3m4 understand and explain basic operations (addition, subtraction, multiplication, division) involving whole numbers by modelling and discussing a variety of problem situations (e.g., show division as sharing, show multiplication as repeated addition)<br>3m7 select and perform computation techniques (addition, subtraction, multiplication, division) appropriate to specific problems and determine whether the results are reasonable<br>3m8 solve problems and describe and explain the variety of strategies used<br>3m9 justify in oral or written expression the method chosen for addition and subtraction, estimation, mental computation, concrete materials, algorithms, calculators<br>3m10 use a calculator to solve problems beyond the required pencil-and-paper skills<br>3m11 read and print numerals from 0 to 1000<br>3m13 count by 1s, 2s, 5s, 10s, and 100s to 1000 using various starting points and by 25s to 1000 using multiples of 25 as starting points<br>3m17 identify and describe numbers to 1000 in real-life situations to develop a sense of number (e.g., tell how high a stack of 1000 pennies would be)<br>3m32 use appropriate strategies (e.g., pencil and paper, calculator, estimation, concrete materials) to solve number problems involving whole numbers<br>3m33 use various estimation strategies (e.g., clustering in tens, rounding to hundreds) to solve problems, then check results for reasonableness | **Number Concepts/Number and Relationships Operations: Number Sense and Number Concepts**<br>GCO A Students will demonstrate number sense and apply number theory concepts.<br><br>*KSCO By the end of grade 3, students will be expected to (i) construct and communicate number meanings, and explore and apply estimation strategies, with respect to whole numbers (iii) read and write whole numbers and demonstrate an understanding of place values (to four places)*<br><br>SCO A2 Estimate the size of numbers to the nearest ten or hundred.<br>SCO A4 Demonstrate an understanding of base-10 groupings (units, tens, hundreds, thousands)<br>SCO A5 Record, model, and interpret numbers up to and including the thousands.<br><br>**Number Concepts/Number and Relationships Operations: Number Sense and Number Operations**<br>GCO B Students will demonstrate operation sense and apply operation principles and procedures in both numeric and algebraic situations.<br><br>*KSCO By the end of grade 3, students will be expected to (i) demonstrate an understanding of the connection between relevant, concrete experiences and the mathematical language and symbolism of four basic operations (iii) create and model problem situations involving whole numbers, using one or more of the four basic operations (iv) apply computational facts and strategies with respect to the four basic operations and model addition and subtraction in situations involving whole numbers* | **Strand: Number (Number Concepts)**<br>SO 1 Count by 2s, 5s, 10s, and 100s to 1000 using random starting points. [CN]<br>SO 2 Estimate, then count the number of objects in a set (0 to 1000) and compare the estimate with the actual number. [C, E]<br>SO 11 Represent and describe numbers to 1000 in a variety of ways. [C, PS, R, T, V] | **Strand: Number (Number Concepts)**<br>• Estimate and then count an increased number of objects in a set, and compare the estimate with the actual number.<br>• Skip count forward and backward by 2s, 5s, 10s, 25s, and 100s to 1000, using starting points that are multiples; and skip count forward using random starting points.<br>• Explore, represent, and describe numbers to 1000 in a variety of ways. |

| Puddle Question | Ontario Expectations | Atlantic Provinces Education Foundation (APEF) Outcomes | Western Canadian Protocol (WCP) Specific Outcomes | British Columbia Integrated Resource Package (IRP) Outcomes |
|---|---|---|---|---|
| | | *(vi) apply estimation techniques to predict and justify the reasonableness of results in relevant problem situations involving whole numbers*<br>*(vii) select and use appropriate computational techniques (including mental, paper-and-pencil, and technological) in given situations*<br><br>SCO B1 Recognize several meanings for multiplication.<br>SCO B4 Solve and create problems involving addition and/or subtraction.<br>SCO B5 Solve and create problems involving multiplication and/or division with small numbers.<br>SCO B6 Add and subtract with and without regrouping (up to and including three-digit numbers).<br>SCO B9 Continue to estimate in addition and subtraction situations.<br>SCO B10 Begin to estimate in multiplication and division situations.<br>SCO B11 Mentally add and subtract two-digit and one-digit numbers.<br>SCO B12 Mentally add and subtract rounded numbers. | | |
| **2. Packing Cookies** | 3m4 understand and explain basic operations (addition, subtraction, multiplication, division) involving whole numbers by modelling and discussing a variety of problem situations (e.g., show division as sharing, show multiplication as repeated addition)<br>3m6 develop proficiency in multiplying and dividing one-digit whole numbers<br>3m8 solve problems and describe and explain the variety of strategies used<br>3m9 justify in oral or written expression the method chosen for addition and subtraction, estimation, mental computation, concrete materials, algorithms, calculators<br>3m23 interpret multiplication and division sentences in a variety of ways (e.g., | **Number Concepts/Number and Relationships Operations: Number Sense and Number Concepts**<br>GCO A Students will demonstrate number sense and apply number theory concepts.<br><br>*KSCO By the end of grade 3, students will be expected to (iii) read and write whole numbers and demonstrate an understanding of place values (to four places)*<br><br>SCO A4 Demonstrate an understanding of base-10 groupings (units, tens, hundreds, thousands).<br>SCO A5 Record, model, and interpret numbers up to and including the thousands. | **Strand: Number (Number Concepts)**<br>SO 11 Represent and describe numbers to 1000 in a variety of ways. [C, PS, R, T, V]<br><br>**Strand: Number (Number Operations)**<br>SO 15 Use manipulatives, diagrams, and symbols with maximum products and dividends to 50 to demonstrate and describe the processes of multiplication and division. [C, PS, V] | **Strand: Number (Number Concepts)**<br>• Explore, represent, and describe numbers to 1000 in a variety of ways.<br><br>**Strand: Number (Number Operations)**<br>• Explore and demonstrate the processes of multiplication and division up to 50, using manipulatives, diagrams, and symbols. |

| Puddle Question | Ontario Expectations | Atlantic Provinces Education Foundation (APEF) Outcomes | Western Canadian Protocol (WCP) Specific Outcomes | British Columbia Integrated Resource Package (IRP) Outcomes |
|---|---|---|---|---|
| | using base ten materials, arrays)<br>3m32 use appropriate strategies (e.g., pencil and paper, calculator, estimation, concrete materials) to solve number problems involving whole numbers | **Number Concepts/Number and Relationships Operations: Number Sense and Number Operations**<br>CGO B Students will demonstrate operation sense and apply operation principles and procedures in both numeric and algebraic situations.<br><br>*KSCO By the end of grade 3, students will be expected to*<br>*(i) demonstrate an understanding of the connection between relevant, concrete experiences and the mathematical language and symbolism of the four basic operations*<br>*(ii) recognize and explain the relationships among the four basic operations*<br>*(iii) create and model problem situations involving whole numbers, using one or more of the four basic operations*<br>*(v) apply computational facts and strategies with respect to the four basic operations and to model addition and subtraction in situations involving whole numbers*<br>*(vii) select and use appropriate computational techniques (including mental, paper-and-pencil, and technological) in given situations*<br><br>SCO B1 Recognize several meanings for multiplication.<br>SCO B2 Recognize several meanings for division.<br>SCO B3 Recognize the relationship between multiplication and division.<br>SCO B5 Solve and create problems involving multiplication and/or division with small numbers.<br>SCO B7 Recognize principles of multiplication and division.<br>SCO B8 Relate multiplication and division facts.<br>SCO B10 Begin to estimate in multiplication and division situations. | | |

| Puddle Question | Ontario Expectations | Atlantic Provinces Education Foundation (APEF) Outcomes | Western Canadian Protocol (WCP) Specific Outcomes | British Columbia Integrated Resource Package (IRP) Outcomes |
|---|---|---|---|---|
| **3. Share With Friends** | 3m4 understand and explain basic operations (addition, subtraction, multiplication, division) involving whole numbers by modelling and discussing a variety of problem situations (e.g., show division as sharing, show multiplication as repeated addition)<br>3m8 solve problems and describe and explain the variety of strategies used<br>3m20 represent and explain common fractions, presented in real-life situations, as part of a whole, part of a set, and part of a measure using concrete materials and drawings (e.g., find one-third of a length of ribbon by folding) | **Number Concepts/Number and Relationships Operations: Number Sense and Number Concepts**<br>GCO A Students will demonstrate number sense and apply number theory concepts.<br><br>*KSCO By the end of grade 3, students will be expected to*<br>*(ii) concretely explore common fractions and decimals in meaningful situations*<br>*(iii) read and write whole numbers and demonstrate an understanding of place values (to four places)*<br><br>SCO A3 Use simple fractions to describe situations.<br>SCO A4 Demonstrate an understanding of base-10 groupings (units, tens, hundreds, thousands).<br><br>**Number Concepts/Number and Relationships Operations: Number Sense and Number Operations**<br>CGO B Students will demonstrate operation sense and apply operation principles and procedures in both numeric and algebraic situations.<br><br>*KSCO By the end of grade 3, students will be expected to*<br>*(i) demonstrate an understanding of the connection between relevant, concrete experiences and the mathematical language and symbolism of the four basic operations*<br>*(ii) recognize and explain the relationships among the four basic operations*<br>*(iii) create and model problem situations involving whole numbers, using one or more of the four basic operations*<br><br>SCO B1 Recognize several meanings for multiplication.<br>SCO B2 Recognize several meanings for division.<br>SCO B3 Recognize the relationship between multiplication and division.<br>SCO B4 Solve and create problems involving addition and/or subtraction. | This problem does not address the grade 3 specific outcomes as stated in the Western Canadian Protocol (WCP) document. | **Strand: Number (Number Concepts)**<br>• Demonstrate and explain in a variety of ways an understanding of halves, thirds, fourths, fifths, and tenths as part of a region or set.<br><br>**Strand: Number (Number Operations)**<br>• Explore and demonstrate the processes of multiplication and division up to 50, using manipulatives, diagrams, and symbols. |

| Puddle Question | Ontario Expectations | Atlantic Provinces Education Foundation (APEF) Outcomes | Western Canadian Protocol (WCP) Specific Outcomes | British Columbia Integrated Resource Package (IRP) Outcomes |
|---|---|---|---|---|
| | | SCO B5 Solve and create problems involving multiplication and/or division with small numbers. | | |
| **4. Measure a Friend** | 3m34 demonstrate an understanding of and ability to apply measurement terms: centimetre, metre, kilometre; millilitre, litre; gram, kilogram; degree Celsius; week, month, year<br>3m36 solve problems related to their day-to-day environment using measurement and estimation (e.g., in finding the height of the school fence)<br>3m37 estimate, measure, and record the perimeter and the area of two-dimensional shapes, and compare the perimeters and areas<br>3m38 estimate, measure, and record the capacity of containers and the mass of familiar objects, and compare the measures<br>3m40 select the most appropriate unit of measure to measure length (centimetre, metre, kilometre)<br>3m41 estimate, measure, and record linear dimensions of objects (using centimetre, metre, kilometre)<br>3m42 compare and order objects by their linear dimensions<br>3m51 measure the perimeter of two-dimensional shapes using standard units (centimetre and metre), and compare the perimeters<br>3m52 estimate and measure the area of shapes using uniform non-standard units, and compare and order the shapes by area<br>3m53 estimate, measure, and record the capacity of containers using standard units (millilitre, litre), and compare the measures<br>3m54 estimate, measure, and record the mass of familiar objects using standard units (gram, kilogram) | **Shape and Space: Measurement**<br>GCO D Students will demonstrate an understanding of, and apply concepts and skills associated with, measurement.<br><br>*KSCO By the end of grade 3, students will be expected to (ii) identify and use non-standard and standard units of measurement and appreciate their role in communication (iii) estimate and determine measurements in everyday problem situations and develop a sense of the relative size of units*<br><br>SCO D1 Estimate and measure length in metres, decimetres, and centimetres.<br>SCO D2 Estimate and measure capacity in millilitres and litres.<br>SCO D3 Estimate and measure mass in grams and kilograms.<br>SCO D4 Estimate and measure area in non-standard units and square centimetres.<br>SCO D6 Use appropriate units for capacity and mass.<br>SCO D8 Continue to solve a wide variety of measurement problems. | **Strand: Shape and Space (Measurement)**<br>SO 1 Select the most appropriate standard unit, including km, to measure length. [E, R, V]<br>SO 3 Estimate, measure, record, compare, and order objects by length, height, and perimeter, using standard units. [E, PS]<br>SO 7 Select an appropriate object or nonstandard unit to measure capacity or volume of a container. [E, V]<br>SO 9 Estimate, measure, record, and compare the mass (weight) of objects, using standard units (g, kg). [E, PS] | **Strand: Shape and Space (Measurement)**<br>• Estimate, measure, record, compare, and order objects and containers using standard and non-standard units.<br>• Select the most appropriate standard unit for measuring length (cm, m, km), mass (g, kg), volume (L), and time (minutes, hours, days). |

| Puddle Question | Ontario Expectations | Atlantic Provinces Education Foundation (APEF) Outcomes | Western Canadian Protocol (WCP) Specific Outcomes | British Columbia Integrated Resource Package (IRP) Outcomes |
|---|---|---|---|---|
| **5. What Can You Buy?** | 3m8 solve problems and describe and explain the variety of strategies used<br>3m29 add and subtract three-digit numbers with and without regrouping using concrete materials<br>3m31 pose and solve number problems involving more than one operation (e.g., if there are 24 students in our class and 5 boys and 9 girls wore boots, how many students did not wear boots?)<br>3m32 use appropriate strategies (e.g., pencil and paper, calculator, estimation, concrete materials) to solve number problems involving whole numbers<br>3m48 demonstrate the relationship between all coins and bills up to $100<br>3m49 make purchases and change for money amounts up to $10, and estimate, count, and record the value up to $10 of a collection of coins and bills<br>3m50 read and write money amounts using two forms of notation (89¢ and $0.89) | **Number Concepts/Number and Relationships Operations: Number Sense and Number Concepts**<br>GCO A Students will demonstrate number sense and apply number theory concepts.<br><br>*KSCO By the end of grade 3, students will be expected to*<br>*(i) construct and communicate number meanings, and explore and apply estimation strategies, with respect to whole numbers*<br>*(iii) read and write whole numbers and demonstrate an understanding of place values (to four places)*<br>*(v) apply number theory concepts, e.g., place-value pattern, in meaningful contexts with respect to whole numbers and commonly used fractions and decimals*<br><br>SCO A2 Estimate the size of numbers to the nearest ten or hundred.<br>SCO A4 Demonstrate an understanding of base-10 groupings (units, tens, hundreds, thousands.)<br>SCO A5 Record, model, and interpret numbers up to and including thousands.<br>SCO A7 Extend the place-value system to model and record numbers involving tenths.<br><br>**Number Concepts/Number and Relationships Operations: Number Sense and Number Operations**<br>CGO B Students will demonstrate operation sense and apply operation principles and procedures in both numeric and algebraic situations.<br><br>*KSCO By the end of grade 3, students will be expected to*<br>*(iii) create and model problem situations involving whole numbers, using one or more of the four basic operations*<br>*(v) apply computational facts and strategies with respect to the four basic operations and to model addition and subtraction in situations involv-* | **Strand: Number (Number Concepts)**<br>SO 6 Recognize, build, compare, and order sets that contain 0 to 100 elements. [PS, R, V]<br>SO 8 Read and write numerals to 1000. [C, CN, V]<br>SO 11 Represent and describe numbers to 1000 in a variety of ways. [C, PS, R, T, V]<br><br>**Strand: Number (Number Operations)**<br>SO 14 Use manipulatives, diagrams, and symbols in a problem solving context to demonstrate and describe the processes of addition and subtraction of numbers to 1000 with and without regrouping. [C, PS, R, V]<br><br>**Strand: Shape and Space (Measurement)**<br>SO 17 Create and recognize that a given value of money can be represented in many different ways. [PS, R]<br>SO 19 Make purchases and change up to $10. [PS] | **Strand: Number (Number Concepts)**<br>• Recognize, build, compare, and order sets that contain 0 to 1000 elements.<br>• Read and write number words to 100 and numerals to 1000.<br>• Explore, represent, and describe numbers to 1000 in a variety of ways.<br><br>**Strand: Number (Operations)**<br>• Demonstrate and describe the processes of addition and subtraction of whole numbers to 1000 with and without regrouping, using manipulatives, diagrams, and symbols.<br><br>**Strand: Shape and Space (Measurement)**<br>• Identify and use coins and bills (to $100) to estimate, count, record collections, create equivalent sets, and make change up to $10.<br>• Read and write both forms of money notation (e.g., 89¢ and $0.89). |

| Puddle Question | Ontario Expectations | Atlantic Provinces Education Foundation (APEF) Outcomes | Western Canadian Protocol (WCP) Specific Outcomes | British Columbia Integrated Resource Package (IRP) Outcomes |
|---|---|---|---|---|
| | | *ing whole numbers*<br>*(vii) select and use appropriate computational techniques (including mental, paper-and-pencil, and technological) in given situations*<br><br>SCO B4 Solve and create problems involving addition and/or subtraction.<br>SCO B5 Solve and create problems involving multiplication and/or division with small numbers.<br>SCO B6 Add and subtract with and without regrouping (up to and including three-digit numbers).<br>SCO B7 Recognize principles of multiplication and division.<br>SCO B8 Relate multiplication and division facts.<br>SCO B9 Continue to estimate in addition and subtraction situations.<br>SCO B10 Begin to estimate in multiplication and division situations.<br>SCO B11 Mentally add and subtract two-digit and one-digit numbers.<br>SCO B12 Mentally add and subtract rounded numbers.<br>SCO B13 Use technology to solve problems involving larger numbers. | | |
| **6. Sort Shapes** | 3m55 investigate the attributes of three-dimensional figures and two-dimensional shapes using concrete materials and drawings<br>3m60 use language effectively to describe geometric concepts, reasoning, and investigations | **Shape and Geometry**<br>GCO E Students will demonstrate spatial sense and apply geometric concepts, properties, and relationships.<br><br>KSCO By the end of grade 3, students will be able to (i) explore and experiment with geometric shapes and relationships | **Strand: Shape and Space (3-D Objects and 2-D Shapes)**<br>SO 22 Identify and count faces, vertices, and edges of 3-D objects. [E]<br>SO 26 Compare and contrast two 3-D objects. [C, CN] | **Strand: Shape and Space (3-D Objects and 2-D Shapes)**<br>• Compare, contrast, sort, and classify two-dimensional shapes and three-dimensional objects using two or more attributes.<br>• Identify, count, and describe the faces, vertices, edges, sides, and angles of polygons and solids. |

| Puddle Question | Ontario Expectations | Atlantic Provinces Education Foundation (APEF) Outcomes | Western Canadian Protocol (WCP) Specific Outcomes | British Columbia Integrated Resource Package (IRP) Outcomes |
|---|---|---|---|---|
| | 3m61 investigate the similarities and differences among a variety of prisms using concrete materials and drawings<br>3m65 compare and sort two-dimensional shapes according to two or more attributes<br>3m66 compare and sort three-dimensional figures according to two or more geometric attributes (e.g., size, number of faces)<br>3m67 describe and name prisms and pyramids by the shape of their base (e.g., square-based pyramid)<br>3m70 explore and identify two-dimensional shapes using concrete materials and drawings (e.g., rhombus, parallelogram) | *(ii) describe, model, draw, and classify 2-D figures and 3-D shapes*<br>*(iv) relate geometric ideas to number and measurement ideas and recognize and apply geometric principles in real-world situations*<br><br>SCO E1 Continue their development of spatial sense with emphasis on perceptual constancy.<br>SCO E5 Recognize, name, describe, and represent different prisms and pyramids.<br>SCO E11 Recognize and identify various polygons, prisms, and pyramids in real-world contexts. | | |
| **7. Shape Game** | 3m57 explore transformations of geometric figures<br>3m59 describe location and movements on a grid<br>3m60 use language effectively to describe geometric concepts, reasoning, and investigations<br>3m74 identify transformations, such as flips, slides, and turns (reflections, translations, and rotations), using concrete materials and drawings<br>3m75 perform rotations using concrete materials (e.g., quarter turn, half turn, three-quarter turn)<br>3m76 describe how to get from one point to another on a grid (e.g., two squares right followed by one square up) | **Patterns and Relations**<br>GCO C Students will explore, recognize, represent, and apply patterns and relationships, both formally and informally.<br><br>*KSCO By the end of grade 3, students will be expected to*<br>*(i) recognize, describe, extend, and create patterns and sequences in a variety of mathematical and real-world contexts, e.g., geometric, numeric, and measurement*<br><br>SCO C2 Recognize and create geometric patterns.<br><br>**Shape and Geometry**<br>GCO E Students will demonstrate spatial sense and apply geometric concepts, properties, and relationships.<br><br>*KSCO By the end of grade 3, students will be expected to*<br>*(i) explore and experiment with geometric shapes and relationships*<br>*(ii) describe, model, draw, and classify 2-D figures and 3-D shapes*<br>*(iv) relate geometric ideas to number and measurement ideas and recognize and* | This problem does not address any of the grade 3 specific outcomes as stated in the Western Canadian Protocol (WCP) document. | **Strand: Shape and Space (Transformations)**<br>• Trace a path on a line following oral or written instructions. |

| Puddle Question | Ontario Expectations | Atlantic Provinces Education Foundation (APEF) Outcomes | Western Canadian Protocol (WCP) Specific Outcomes | British Columbia Integrated Resource Package (IRP) Outcomes |
|---|---|---|---|---|
| | | *apply geometric principles in real-world situations*<br><br>SCO E2 Recognize and represent angles that are less/more than right angles.<br>SCO E3 Recognize, name, describe, and represent congruent angles and congruent polygons.<br>SCO E4 Recognize, name, describe, and represent kites, and some concave, convex, and regular polygons.<br>SCO E10 Recognize, name, describe, and represent half and quarter turns of 2-D figures. | | |
| **8. Pattern Game** | 3m78 identify, extend, and create linear and non-linear geometric patterns, number and measurement patterns, and patterns in their environment<br>3m81 understand patterns in which operations are repeated (e.g., multiplication), transformations are repeated, or multiple changes are made to attributes<br>3m84 discuss the choice of a pattern rule<br>3m86 use addition and subtraction facts to generate simple patterns in a hundreds chart<br>3m88 identify relationships between addition, subtraction, multiplication, and division | CGO B Students will demonstrate operation sense and apply operation principles and procedures in both numeric and algebraic situations.<br><br>*KSCO By the end of grade 3, students will be expected to (iii) create and model problem situations involving whole numbers, using one or more of the four basic operations (vii) select and use appropriate computational techniques (including mental, paper-and-pencil, and technological) in given situations*<br><br>SCO B4 Solve and create problems involving addition and/or subtraction.<br>SCO B5 Solve and create problems involving multiplication and/or division with small numbers.<br>SCO B11 Mentally add and subtract two-digit and one-digit numbers.<br><br>**Patterns and Relations**<br>GCO C Students will explore, recognize, represent, and apply patterns and relationships, both formally and informally.<br><br>*KSCO By the end of grade 3, students will be expected to (i) recognize, describe, extend, and create patterns and sequences in a variety of mathematical and real-world* | **Strand: Patterns and Relations (Patterns)**<br>SO 2 Use objects and concrete models to explain the rule for a pattern, such as those found on addition and multiplication charts. [C, R, V]<br><br>**NOTE:** The grade 2 outcome SO 4 is subsumed in this task.<br>SO 4 Create, extend and describe patterns, including numerical and non-numerical patterns [C, CN, PS] | **Strand: Patterns and Relations**<br>• Identify, create, and describe number and non-number patterns.<br>• Explain the rule for a pattern and make predictions based on patterns using models and objects. |

| Puddle Question | Ontario Expectations | Atlantic Provinces Education Foundation (APEF) Outcomes | Western Canadian Protocol (WCP) Specific Outcomes | British Columbia Integrated Resource Package (IRP) Outcomes |
|---|---|---|---|---|
| | | *contexts, e.g., geometric, numeric, and measurement*<br>*(ii) use patterns to solve problems*<br><br>SCO C1 Recognize the pattern implicit in the place-value system.<br>SCO C2 Recognize and create geometric patterns.<br>SCO C3 Use and recognize the patterns in the multiplication table. | | |
| **9. Milkshake Flavours** | 3m90 sort, classify, and cross-classify objects and data<br>3m92 interpret displays of data, present the information, and discuss it using mathematical language<br>3m99 relate objects to number on a graph with many-to-one correspondence (e.g., 1 Canadian flag represents 100 Canadian citizens)<br>3m101 construct bar graphs (with discrete classes on one axis and number on the other) and pictographs using scales with multiples of 2, 5, and 10<br>3m102 interpret data from graphs (e.g., bar graphs, pictographs, and circle graphs) | **Data Management and Probability: Data Management**<br>GCO F Students will solve problems involving the collection, display, and analysis of data.<br><br>*KSCO By the end of grade 3, students will be expected to*<br>*(i) collect, record, organize, and describe relevant data*<br>*(ii) construct concrete and pictorial displays of relevant data*<br>*(iii) read and interpret displays of relevant data*<br><br>SCO F1 Select appropriate strategies for collecting, recording, organizing, and describing relevant data.<br>SCO F2 Interpret and create pictographs in which each symbol represents more than one item. | **Strand: Statistics and Probability (Data Analysis)**<br>SO 3 Display the same data in more than one way. [PS]<br><br>**NOTE:** The grade 2 outcomes, SO 4 and SO 5, are also subsumed in this task.<br>SO 4 Construct and label concrete/object graphs, pictographs, and bar graphs. [PS, V]<br>SO 5 Discuss data, and draw and communicate appropriate conclusions. [C, R] | **Strand: Statistics and Probability (Data Analysis)**<br>• Display data in more than one way, including graphs, pictographs, bar graphs, and rank ordering.<br>• Discuss data, communicate conclusions, and make predictions and inferences to solve similar problems. |
| **10. Who Will Win?** | 3m93 demonstrate an understanding of probability and demonstrate the ability to apply probability in familiar day-to-day situations<br>3m103 conduct simple probability experiments (e.g., rolling a number cube, spinning a spinner) and predict the results<br>3m104 apply the concept of likelihood of events in solving simple problems<br>3m106 use mathematical language (e.g., possible, impossible) in discussion to describe probability | **Data Management and Probability: Probability**<br>GCO G Students will represent and solve problems involving uncertainty.<br><br>*KSCO By the end of grade 3, students will be expected to*<br>*(i) conduct informal investigations of chance and estimate probabilities with respect to games and other simple, everyday situations*<br><br>SCO G1 Predict and record results in experiments using spinners, coins, dice, coloured cubes, and other simple equipment. | **Strand: Statistics and Probability (Chance and Uncertainty)**<br>SO 6 Describe the likelihood of an outcome, using such terms as more likely, less likely, chance. [C, R]<br>SO 7 Conduct a probability experiment, choose an appropriate recording method, and draw conclusions from the results. [C, E, PS] | **Strand: Statistics and Probability (Chance and Uncertainty)**<br>• Describe the likeliness of an outcome using terms such as likely, unlikely, fair chance, probable, and expected.<br>• Conduct a probability experiment, choose an appropriate recording method, and draw conclusions and make predictions from the results. |